"Ken is easily one of the greatest prospectors in the sales profession. I have watched him apply his craft for over a decade. The book is fantastic. A must read for any sales person or networker!"

~Orjan Saele – Founder, Zinzino Inc., Oslo, Norway

"Ken Dunn does a great job conveying the six timeless secrets of successful prospecting, and he does it through the story of Laura Dunagan. Every secret is illustrated through her struggles. Laura is a young lady we can all relate to. Her father was a prospector, and she was absolutely determined to follow in his footsteps. But life dealt her a cruel twist and forever shattered her dream of prospecting ... or did it? She did become *The Greatest Prospector In The World*, but you'll have to read Ken's book to find out how."

~John Haremza – Bestselling Author of
I'm Going to the Top and *Right or Almost Right*

"This book is absolutely a hands-down must read for anyone in sales, including entrepreneurs and all business people. Learning about the six secrets Ken teaches is something you won't want to miss. Each one is essential to success."

~Esther Spina – Bestselling Author of
The Ambitious Woman and *The Everthing Guide To Network Marketing*

"*The Greatest Prospector In The World* is a POWERFUL book that every aspiring networker and salesperson must read! Engaging read, with tons of lessons."

~Jordan Adler – International Bestselling Author of
Beach Money

"Ken Dunn has created an enchanting tale that incorporates the classic tools of transformation into a few simple rules for reaching one's fullest potential in business and in life. Truly a delightful book that can change your life."

~ Thomas Tidlund – Entrepreneur & Networker, Zinzino Sweden

"Ken does a masterful job of catching your heart through this whimsical story that he uses to deliver sage advice on sales. A must read for anyone that is looking for new customers."

~ Donna Johnson – International Business Consultant, Arbonne International

THE
GREATEST
PROSPECTOR
IN THE WORLD

THE GREATEST PROSPECTOR IN THE WORLD

A Historically Accurate Parable on
Creating Success in Sales, Business & Life

KEN DUNN

NEXT CENTURY
PUBLISHING

Acknowledgements

This book is dedicated to two of the most amazing people that I've ever met in my life. Matthew and Laura, you have both inspired me to pursue my dreams and I will never be able to properly thank you for this. I love you both with all my heart.

To my best friend, my confidant, my biggest supporter and the love of my life: Julie, I will take any opportunity I can to thank you and express how much I love you.

Finally, I want to thank the incredible team at Next Century Publishing. This book would not have turned out so amazing if it were not for the part that each of you played in the project.

Table of Contents

Foreword

Ken Dunn is one of the greatest prospectors in the sales profession. Had he chosen to write a manual based on his prospecting principles, it would have sold around the world. Ken, however, has raised the bar for all salespeople, including himself. When timeless principles are married to a compelling storyline, classic literature is the result. Indeed, *The Greatest Prospector In The World* is an instant sales classic. Ken entertains the reader while intertwining his mastery of the sales process throughout this educational and historical work of fiction. Of course, this is exactly what Ken intended since he understands that "facts tell, but stories sell."

Importantly, Ken doesn't just explain these principles—he has lived them. Armed with only a high school education, Ken has successfully started numerous businesses in various industries, including property management, finance, direct sales, and publishing. Despite wildly different business models, Ken's prospecting and sales expertise, combined with an unquenchable drive, has led to revenue growth wherever he goes. Thus, the six prospecting principles taught in *The Greatest Prospector In The World* are applicable no matter the field of business. Ken has outlined the recipe for sales success; the reader must now add his or her hunger to the mix.

I have known Ken personally for nearly a decade, and I know of no individual who is better at the prospecting process. I believe every person has unique skills and talents. Unfortunately, only a few courageously discipline themselves to share their gifts in order to bless others. Ken is one of them. Through the inspiration received by blockbuster hits such as Jim Stovall's *Ultimate Life* series and Og Mandino's *The Greatest Salesman in the World*, he has blessed all of us by writing *The Greatest Prospector In The World*. It's time to turn the page and learn how you too can be the world's greatest prospector.

~Orrin Woodward, Inc. Magazine Top 20 Leader, NY Times Bestselling Author, and Chairman of the Board, LIFE Leadership

THE
GREATEST
PROSPECTOR
IN THE WORLD

1

Exile

Denver Union Station, 1910

"GOING FISHING, YOUNG LADY?"

The question came from a strange man wearing a tweed suit and a black bowler hat. He had taken a seat at the counter of the diner, a couple of stools down from me, glanced across, and done a double take, no doubt at the sight of a sixteen-year-old girl dressed as I was.

"No, sir," I replied, without turning to look at him.

"What's with the waders, then?"

"What's it to you?" I scooped up some whipped cream from my chocolate malt with my long spoon.

 The man did not respond. Instead, he drank his coffee in silence and watched the cooks make our breakfast. I glanced across the diner to where my Uncle Joe and my older brother

Matthew sat in a booth, tucking in to their breakfasts. I'd elected to sit alone at the counter, not wanting to have to make conversation with them. But I didn't mind talking to the stranger. For some reason, I felt like this kind-faced man with the neatly trimmed, bushy brown mustache and matching sideburns deserved an explanation as to why a sixteen-year-old girl would be sitting in a train station diner in Denver, Colorado, dressed in bib overalls, rubber waders, and a wide-brimmed hat.

"I'm a prospector."

"Excuse me?"

"I'm a prospector from Fairbanks, Alaska."

He put down his coffee cup and gave me his full attention. "Prospector? You mean, like a panning-for-gold kind of prospector?"

"Yep." I sat up a little straighter on my red vinyl stool. "I've been panning and prospecting for gold my whole life."

"How old are ya?"

"Sixteen. My dad's the best prospector in Alaska, as were his dad and his grandfather before him. I'm a fourth-generation gold prospector. I started panning for gold when I was six years old."

Uncle Joe was watching me from across the room. When I looked his way, he tipped his hat and smiled.

The stranger nodded toward him. "Is that your father?"

At this moment, the server delivered my pancakes, and I was glad of an excuse to turn away so the stranger wouldn't see the tears that sprang to my eyes.

"No. That's my Uncle Joe, my dad's brother. He's taking me and my brother, Matthew to live with him in Chicago. My dad died last week—in a mining accident."

* * * * *

I had known the moment I arrived home from school on that terrible day that something was wrong. Trudging down the logging road that led to our little cabin, I'd been enjoying the feeling of newly thawed mud beneath my black boots and the sounds of spring stirring in the forest. I turned the corner on Cracker Hollow and spotted our cabin, nestled on the hillside, with a light covering of snow on the rooftop. I was looking forward to our afternoon routine: Dad would have come home for lunch and stoked the fire, adding a few logs to ensure the temperature was perfect. When the smoke from the chimney came into view, I'd sprint home. Once inside, I would rush through my homework, finish my chores, then grab my waders and scramble down the trail with Dad to go prospecting—the thing I loved most in the world.

But that day there was no smoke.

I paused. *Something's wrong!* In a panic, I ran the last half-mile home, threw open the door, tossed my books on the kitchen table and yelled, "Dad?"

The cabin was cold and silent. I checked the mudroom, the loft, the bedrooms, the ramshackle outhouse. He was nowhere in sight. His noonday sandwiches, carrots, and apple, which I had prepared for him that morning, were still sitting on the marble shelf in the larder. A lead weight settled in my stomach.

The river.

I ran out of the cabin, forgetting my waders, my mind churning out thoughts like a steamboat churns through a river. Maybe Dad hit a main artery and found nuggets the size of golf balls . . . maybe a piece of equipment broke down and Dad had to fix it . . . maybe . . .

At the riverbank, I came to a dead stop. Nothing. Overwhelmed with dread, I screamed, "Dad!"

No answer.

"Wait a minute," I said aloud, relief flooding through me, "Dad's prospecting just south of the gorge today!"

Off I sprinted, down the rutted trail that ran beside the river. "Dad! Dad!" I yelled, as I scrambled over the rugged terrain, clutching renewed hope close to my fast-beating heart. With half a mile to go, I could hear men's voices, and I headed toward them. Clambering over a couple of boulders and pushing through the last branches, I burst out into a clearing and peered across the river. A dozen men were working close to the opposite bank, digging away rocks, debris, and rubble.

"Keep digging, boys; he's gotta be in there!"

"Can you hear anything?" someone asked.

"Billy, are you there?" a huge man in a red lumberjack jacket yelled.

I stood on the bank, dumbfounded. The frantic clashing of metal on rock stung my ears. The man in the lumberjack jacket dropped his shovel and grabbed a rope

hanging from the saddle of a nearby horse. After wrapping it around a large boulder, he secured the other end to the saddle horn, and yelled, "Yah!" smacking the horse's rump. The horse strained to move forward, guided by another man.

It didn't feel real. But when I saw Dad's coffee thermos and his prospecting tools, it hit me: *My dad is underneath those rocks!* Without thinking twice, I plunged into the icy water.

* * * * *

They finally dug his body out just before midnight. Our neighbor, Mrs. Oliver, who'd been like a mother to me since mine died, had taken me home and got me into dry clothes. There was no point in freezing there by the river while the men worked by lamplight. I'd understood, by then, that there was little hope, but I couldn't accept it. Dad was the best prospector in the state, and there was no way he would have failed to recognize the danger signs of loose boulders or unstable walls. He had taught me safety tips from the time I was knee high, and one of them was to know the density and depth of a cliff or a mine before tapping into its core. "Don't let greed cause you to fail to trust the rocks—the rocks never lie," he always said. How could he have forgotten? How could he have not listened?

Arriving back at the cabin, the trees, the house, the trails, the woodpile, and the yard all blurred, and I saw only the smoke-less chimney. As I opened the front door, reality set in—I was all alone. My school bag was lying on the floor, and I knew Dad's lunch was still in the pantry. The entire house felt cold, damp, and eerie. In my mind, I could hear Dad's voice reminding me that we should try to keep the stove fired up all the time: "A warm, dry house is the way your mother liked it," he would tell me. But she was gone. She had died of cancer when I was only four years old. And now he was gone too.

* * * * *

"I'm sorry."

It seemed as if I'd been silent for hours, lost in painful memories while my pancakes went cold, but in reality it couldn't have been more than a couple of minutes. The kind-faced stranger had been quiet too, but now his soft words snapped me back to the present—to the shiny chrome counter, the smell of frying bacon, the noise of trains pulling in and out of the station.

He seemed to sense that I didn't want to say more about the accident, so he asked: "How did you and your dad end up being prospectors in Alaska?"

"My dad's grandpa, Papa James, started prospecting in San Francisco during the Gold Rush," I replied. My dad used to tell me stories about Papa James and his prospecting adventures at night in our cabin. I knew our family history better than anything I'd learned in school.

"Before Papa James died, he left his fortune to his two sons, Pop Angus and Uncle Jack, but Uncle Jack died and Pop Angus ended up with all the inheritance." I paused.

"Pop Angus had married an Indian woman from one of the Washington tribes, and he had two sons—my dad and Uncle Joe. She died of smallpox when they were very young. Pop invested all of his inheritance in bonds with Northern Pacific Railway, but they went bankrupt. He was forced to sell his farm, and got a job on a fishing boat, harpooning whales and netting salmon off the southern coast of Alaska. One day, he was dining in a local pub in Sitka, a coastal town on the southern peninsula of Alaska, when he overheard a group of Russian fishermen talking about how some prospectors had found gold in nearby streams.

"That night, Pop dug out a notebook that his father, Papa James, had used to pen his tales of San Francisco and his ideas for success in the prospecting business. He read over the notebook long into the night, and the love of gold was born in his heart."

I paused to check on my uncle and brother, who were still deep in conversation, and took a bite of my pancakes. The stranger waited for me to continue, a polite smile tugging at his lips beneath his mustache. "When Pop Angus returned to Seattle, he told my dad and Uncle Joe about the gold. He told them about Papa James's notebook, which contained six secrets of success for prospecting, and declared that he wanted to move to Sitka to pan for gold.

"When they got there, they quickly realized that news of the Sitka gold discovery had spread, drawing hundreds if not thousands of prospectors. Most of them failed, due to a lack of funds, shelter, or prospecting experience. Some headed back home, while others fell ill under the harsh weather conditions, and many of them died.

"But not Pop. Dad told me they followed Papa James's instructions and, sure 'nough, they found gold—several ounces after just three weeks of prospecting. Over the next few months they kept succeeding, but the influx of prospectors made it difficult, and disputes over land and location became an issue."

I paused for a long moment, eating my pancakes.

"You have quite a story," the man said. "You're gonna tell me the rest, aren't you?"

"Sure." I stuffed another forkful into my mouth, and continued. "About that time, news came of gold discoveries in Dawson City. Pop decided to move there and continue prospecting. That's when everything changed. Uncle Joe, for some reason I still don't know, left my dad and Pop Angus. He took his portion of their earnings and moved to Chicago. Pop and Dad went to Dawson City. That's where my dad met my mom, Mary.

"Pop Angus and Dad continued to pan for gold and things were going well, until Pop got frostbite in his feet. Dad said it was so bad that his feet needed to be amputated, but Pop refused. Infection set in and he died.

"After they buried my granddad, Dad heard news of gold further north in Fairbanks, Alaska, that was bringing thousands of new prospectors from Seattle and California. He decided to move on again. He purchased a cabin in the hills near Tanana Valley on the Tanana River. The terrain up there was so rough that not many prospectors ventured that far. Dad said that if you didn't have a team of dogs or some mules, getting out there was almost impossible. It didn't stop the gold stampede, but Dad was the best prospector of them all, and we were comfortable out in the wilderness.

"My mom died when I was four, so then it was just me, my dad, and my brother, Matthew—that's him over there with Uncle Joe." I jerked my head toward the booth.

"Is he a prospector too?" the man asked.

I shook my head emphatically. Matthew, who was four years older than me, had never wanted to get into the family business. "Don't mean nothin' to me," he'd say. Not the river, the excitement, the family tradition, not even the gold. He had greater plans that did not involve the mountains or rivers. He left home right after high school and moved to Anchorage to pursue a career in engineering. So then it was just Dad and me, living on top of Beaver Creek Mountain, in the middle of nowhere, surrounded by gold-rich rivers and streams.

Unlike Matthew, I had dreamed of continuing the family business since I was a little girl. There were tons of gold in the mine at Crow's Creek—or so everyone said. Dad had proclaimed there was enough gold for everyone to get filthy rich, and I was determined to get my share. Usually, I'd mine a few ounces each week in the little time I had after school. I couldn't wait till I was old enough to leave behind those pointless books and tests and join Dad full-time. That was the plan. That was how my life was supposed to happen—until I'd been uprooted from the home I loved by Uncle Joe, Dad's brother. Uncle Joe, whom I'd never met until last week, when he showed up at Dad's funeral with his carefully curled mustache and perfectly trimmed sideburns, his three-piece suit and his gold pocket watch, driving a fancy automobile.

Dad had never talked about Uncle Joe. All I knew about him was what I'd told the stranger, that he'd abandoned the family and moved to Chicago. Which was where he was taking us now, despite my desperate pleas to stay in the home I loved. My last act of rebellion had been to insist on wearing my bib overalls and waders, and on bringing along my prospecting pan and Dad's tools in the green duffel bag he'd always carried to work. They could take me away from my home, but they couldn't take away who I was.

I looked up at the clock. It was almost time to board the train. But surprisingly, talking to this stranger was doing me some good. I was almost feeling normal again, for the first time since Dad's accident.

Just then, Matthew tapped me on the shoulder. "Hey kid, you ready to go?" He was all dressed up like a banker, with a bow tie, vest, and coat. Irritated, I ignored him and kept eating my pancakes. He'd protested at my outfit when I came downstairs that morning, but I thought he looked much more ridiculous, trying to dress just like Uncle Joe.

My companion nodded at Matthew and said good morning to Uncle Joe as he walked by. Uncle Joe smiled at him as he moved toward the front door. How strange—it seemed as if they knew each other.

Stiff and tired, I finally pushed off the stool, adjusted the straps to my bib overalls, and shook the boots of my waders. "It was nice talking to ya, mister."

"Same here." Then the man swiveled on his stool and faced me. "By the way, I didn't get your name."

"Laura. Laura Jewel Dunagan." I stood up straight and put on my hat.

He reached out his hand to shake mine. "Dale. Dale Carnegie."

"Nice to meet you, Mr. Carnegie." I walked a few steps, then stopped and turned my head over my shoulder. "Mr. Carnegie?"

"Yes?"

"Remember my name, because someday I'll be famous and rich, and everyone will call me *The Greatest Prospector In The World!*"

He chuckled. "Sure thing, kid. And remember this: no matter what happens, always be yourself."

I took my seat on the train and looked out the window in time to see Mr. Carnegie exit the diner. He walked up to the train attendant and showed him his ticket, and as he passed our carriage, he looked up and saw me in the window. He smiled, tipped his hat, and mouthed the words again: "Be yourself."

2

Heritage

BE YOURSELF. Well, this train was certainly not my style. Taking my seat and defiantly putting my booted feet on the table, I was struck again by the luxury that surrounded me. I'd never ridden on a train be‑fore yesterday, and had been taken by sur‑prise when we boarded. It was nothing like I had imagined. It looked like the hotel lobby in town, but nicer. The walls  were covered with elaborate wallpaper. Curtains of deep red crushed velvet hung at the windows. The seats were high-backed and covered with white leather. A cart full of fresh fruit and vegetables, a chrome coffee pot, fine china, and crystal glasses was secured to one wall, and a butler came with hot moist towels to wipe our hands and feet. I snatched my hands away.

I liked my nails just the way they were—with good ol' mining dirt stuck in them.

There was no one else in the car—just me, Matthew, and Uncle Joe. I did not find out until much later that Uncle Joe had purchased every seat in first class so that the three of us would be alone. I wished that even the two of them were gone—their laughter and endless talking irritated me. As the train rolled out of Denver Union Station and gathered speed, I sank back into the seat farthest from them, the heavy cloud of anger and sadness and hopelessness settling over me once more.

My legs were beginning to sweat from the heat of the rubber waders, but I would be damned if I'd take them off. I picked up my duffel bag and took out the pan and a small hammer that Dad had given me. Closing my eyes, I clutched the familiar tools and tried to bring back the feeling of the river swirling around my waders as Dad and I panned for gold. I could almost feel the pull of the current against my thighs, hear the gurgling of the water, and smell the fresh pine scent of spring. I remembered the times when I had slipped and fallen, and how Dad was always right there to grab me and get me on my feet before I was carried away downstream. I recalled the excitement that brought us back, day after day, rain or shine, never tiring of the search for gold. I'd be back there, one day, doing what I loved most.

I peeked at Uncle Joe and Matthew out of the corner of my eye. They were laughing about something and my anger flared again. Uncle Joe had deserted the family business once, and now he was taking Matthew and me away, putting an end to a long history of prospecting as if it were nothing. *Didn't he care? Had he forgotten the traditions passed down to us?* I wondered what Dad would say. Or what his dad, my grandpa, would think. I was determined not to forget my heritage. One day, it would be up to me to pass down the stories and lessons of successful prospecting to my kids.

Then I heard Uncle Joe say, "Yep, that was good old Papa James." His voice had taken on a faraway tone, and for a moment, he almost sounded like Dad on those winter nights when we would gather around the potbelly stove and he'd tell us spellbinding stories about Papa James, Pop Angus, and the Gold Rush. I kept my head turned toward the window, pretending to admire the view, so the men wouldn't notice that I was suddenly listening intently.

"So Uncle Bobby was the first one to find gold?" Matthew asked.

I stifled a snort of disbelief. Matthew was never very interested back when Dad told these stories. He always seemed bored. But now he was hanging on Uncle Joe's every word, as if he'd never heard the family history before.

"Sure was," Uncle Joe replied. "He was Papa James's cousin, Robert Dunagan, but your dad always called him Uncle Bobby. He lived in San Francisco and worked as a construction laborer in Colma."

I kept my nose glued to the window, but I wasn't seeing the vast plains of the Midwest that stretched away from the track. I was imagining Uncle Bobby in California, more than fifty years ago—a time and a place where gold nuggets were as plentiful as pinecones in Alaska—well, almost. I'd heard this story many times before, but I never tired of it. And Uncle Joe was about to get to the good part.

"One morning, Uncle Bobby was digging trenches for the foundations of a sawmill, when he noticed some shiny metal nuggets in the soil. After further inspection, the foreman, Marshall, and the landowner, Sutter, concluded that it was, indeed, gold. As crazy as it sounds, Mr. Sutter had no interest in gold. In fact, he feared the attention would hinder his plans and the development of his sawmill and farm. But despite Sutter's effort to keep the gold discovery quiet, the news leaked to a local newspaper.

"From there, it spread like wildfire to the East Coast and the *New York Herald* printed the story. Soon, immigrants from around the world invaded San Francisco, lured by the promise of riches. The first year, just a small number of people arrived, probably fewer than five hundred. But by January of 1850, ninety thousand people had descended on Northern California."

Uncle Bobby was one of the early ones, I knew. And he'd sent a telegram to his cousin, Papa James, who was living in the small village of Duwamp on the Duwamish River in Washington State, asking him to come to San Francisco and join him as a prospector. Papa James didn't hesitate for a moment. Aged 41, he left his wife, Grandma Theo, and their two sons, Angus and Jack, behind while he went to seek his fortune. He lived with Uncle Bobby in a small, one-bedroom apartment, where they concealed their findings in the ash-filled stove.

Out of the corner of my eye, I saw Uncle Joe stand up, walk over to the cart, and pour himself a cup of tea. He didn't so much as glance in my direction as he added a splash of milk and turned back to Matthew, stirring his cup idly with a tiny silver spoon. Then he sat back down.

"The gold rush was exciting, but it also brought on many difficulties, hardships and losses. Mining techniques were undeveloped then and many of the prospectors were novices, which caused frequent accidents. Daily disputes ended in deadly arguments. Outbreaks, such as malaria and scarlet fever, along with poor hygiene, led to countless deaths.

"I'm sure Papa James had no idea what he was getting into, but he was a risk-taker. On his first trip, he found so much gold that, when he cashed in his treasures, he returned to Duwamp and purchased a new home and the adjunct general store, which his sons would help run, as a business investment for his mother, Blanche Dunagan, now a widow.

"When he finally returned to San Francisco, the town didn't look the same. Masses of immigrants crowded the streets. What had once been a small town of about a thousand people had turned, almost overnight, into a bustling city of twenty-five thousand. Feuds and disputes were so common that mining without a gun was suicidal. Foreign prospectors had overtaken many of the locations where Uncle Bobby and Papa had previously mined."

Sitting so close to the window, I was getting hot in my overalls and boots. But I didn't dare move; I didn't want the men to think I was listening. I snuck a peek at them, but they weren't looking at me. Quickly, I pulled off my boots, then stuck my nose against the glass again. It sure felt good to wiggle my toes in the fresh air!

Uncle Joe was now telling the part about how Uncle Bobby and Papa James moved into the northern hills, where Uncle Bobby's Mexican wife and her family had lived for decades, and started prospecting in the streams that other prospectors didn't know about. They amassed great quantities of gold, which they kept hidden, but one day, they brought some of the gold into town to exchange it for cash, concealed under deer hides and covered neatly with stacks of lumber, in two wagons disguised as lumber transports. First, though, they attended a public fight between a bull and a black bear, joining a huge crowd of drunken miners who were watching the bloody spectacle unfold in the pit below. Dad had always skipped rather quickly over this part of the story, but Uncle Joe was telling it in gruesome detail—so much so that you'd think he'd been there himself.

"The first bull was dehorned, and the bear made short work of him. The people in the crowd were frustrated, feeling they weren't getting their money's worth. They'd paid a dollar each to see a real fight! They noticed a young, angry bull with long horns in the nearby pen, and began to demand that he take the next turn in the ring. The mounted livestock handlers, known as *vaqueros*, protested—they didn't want their valuable bear killed. But suddenly a hundred revolvers were drawn and pointed in their direction to enforce the request. The *vaqueros* knew that if they didn't release the bull, the black bear would be shot. There was no alternative but to comply; either way, the bear would die.

"Papa James said the bear didn't seem to realize he was in danger. He was accustomed to bulls without horns, so he just stood up as if to hug the charging bull. But one of its horns pierced his abdomen, driving him to the ground. The bear was pinned on its back, but it held the bull tightly, ripping off its ear and inflicting terrible gashes with its claws. Papa said he'd never heard such a bloodcurdling sound as that bull's cries."

Matthew stood up, interrupting the story just as it was getting exciting. His face looked slightly green. "Hold on, Uncle Joe. I gotta go to the bathroom."

Darn, I cussed under my breath. *Can't he handle a little blood? It's just a story, after all.* Sometimes it seemed like Matthew was more girly than I was—and I was the girl! I wanted to hear the part about how the bull broke through the fence and charged through the crowd and off into town with the *vaqueros* in hot pursuit.

"Laura, you want to follow me?"

I breathed a heavy sigh, realizing that I did need to go. I stood up and pulled my boots back on.

"I guess that means yes, Matthew," said Uncle Joe, with a twinkle in his eye. "Take the lady down the hall."

When we returned, I took a seat a little closer to Uncle Joe and Matthew, but continued to feign disinterest as Uncle Joe finished the story, telling of the bull's escape. "Papa said he only stopped when he reached the clothing stores and saw a bright red shirt in the window. He charged the store and did a lot of damage before they eventually roped him and took him back to the pen, where he succeeded in killing the bear, to the delight of the bloodthirsty crowd."

Closing my eyes, I took a deep breath and could almost smell the sweat and the dust and the excitement. It wasn't exactly that I would want to see such an event—I felt bad for the bull and the bear. But that world of toughened men and dirt and danger felt like my world. It was where I came from, and it was real—not like this shiny world of giggling women in fancy dresses and men in suits, riding in luxury trains and automobiles.

I kept my eyes closed, holding on to the sights and smells in my mind, as Uncle Joe's voice picked up the story again.

"Papa James and Uncle Bobby were enjoying being back in town after weeks out in the hills. They decided to visit a local saloon, leaving some of their hired Mexican guards to watch the wagons. Drink was flowing and everyone was in high spirits. And then, a brawl broke out around the poker table, which quickly escalated. Uncle Bobby and Papa James gathered their remaining comrades and exited out of a bedroom window. But when they reached the place where they had left their wagons, the guards were lying face down on the ground in a pool of blood and the wagons were gone.

"Fleeing the town on horseback, they met an angry mob, armed with rifles, blocking the road. Papa James, Uncle Bobby, and their remaining Mexican men spun the horses and galloped off in the opposite direction, bullets whistling in their ears.

"Papa always told me that for some reason, in the panic of the moment, he started laughing and couldn't stop. Afterward, he could never remember what was so funny. But when he looked over at Uncle Bobby, who was also buckled down over his horse's neck, he started laughing all the louder. And then Uncle Bobby suddenly lurched forward. His head drooped and began bobbing up and down lifelessly. He'd been shot!"

"Shot?" asked Matthew. "Uncle Bobby got shot?"

Don't you know anything about our family history? I thought, irritated again. *Of course Uncle Bobby got shot. Were you asleep when Dad told this story?*

The train jerked to a halt, brakes screeching. Uncle Joe smiled. "Yup. Uncle Bobby got shot. But that's another story for another time. Do you kids want to get off the train and stretch your legs?"

We had reached St. Louis. Without answering Uncle Joe, I jammed my feet into my waders, picked up my duffle bag, checked to make sure everything was in it, buckled it shut, and stomped to the door.

Once outside, I stopped abruptly, taken aback by the mass of people with suitcases crowding the platform and exiting and boarding the cars behind the first class coach. I noticed a few women wearing long, puffy dresses and bonnets and holding umbrellas as it started to rain. They were staring in my direction, whispering and laughing. I really didn't care if they thought my waders, bib overalls, and brimmed hat were inappropriate for first class. Frankly, I thought they looked dimwitted in their bonnets. But they continued to gawk and giggle. I decided to take action and stalked toward them.

As I marched in their direction, I noticed a muddy puddle close to where they were standing and had an impulse I couldn't resist. As soon as I reached the puddle, I jumped straight up in the air and landed with both feet right in the middle of it. The women stood with their mouths open. "Looks like you ladies could use some waders," I replied, as they exclaimed in horror over the muddy specks on their dresses. I turned then and walked back to the first class train car, my head held high, a smile spreading across my face, and my step light.

* * * * *

Back on the train, I sat down on a plush footstool and looked out the window at the commotion. The women were talking agitatedly to some railroad attendants dressed in dark suits and dark hats. Uncle Joe and Matthew appeared, with soda pop bottles in their hands. One of the train attendants stopped Uncle Joe and pointed to the women, obviously telling him what had happened. I watched him go to the women, say a few words, and then reach into his coat pocket, remove his long, black wallet, and hand them some money. He tipped his hat to them and headed back to the train.

I pulled Dad's hat over my eyes, hoping Uncle Joe hadn't noticed me watching, leaned my head against the window and pretended to be asleep. A few moments later, I heard the train whistle blow and the jerking movement announced that we were leaving St. Louis. *Not soon enough for me*, I thought as I felt the car pull forward. I peeked out from under my hat, and was mortified to see the butler, on his hands and knees, scrubbing my muddy footprints from the carpet. Uncle Joe and Matthew were in their seats, and Matthew glared at me. I quickly closed my eyes and sank back down under my hat.

Sometime later, the door opened, and the smell of food wafted toward me. I sure was hungry, but I was not going to give Uncle Joe and Matthew the satisfaction of having my company. Soon, I could hear them eating enthusiastically. They didn't even try to rouse me. *Don't they care at all?* My world was collapsing and they were just happily eating dinner in this ridiculous hotel-on-rails. A few minutes later, I heard the butler clearing the dishes. Then he closed the door behind him, and Uncle Joe continued his tale.

"Okay, now where was I?"

"Uncle Bobby had been shot," Matthew reminded him.

"Oh, yes. So Papa grabbed the reins of Uncle Bobby's horse and dragged his limp body over the front of his own saddle, then rode home as fast as he could. Uncle Bobby had lost some blood, but luckily the bullet had only grazed his upper right shoulder. And fortunately for him, Uncle Bobby had consumed enough alcohol that he did not feel a thing. Papa said he slept through the night like a newborn baby."

"Did they ever find the gold?" Matthew asked.

"A few days later, the transport wagons were spotted in a ravine about ten miles from town. But the gold was long gone. Turns out the tavern where the wagons were abducted was called *El Dorado*, owned by the notorious Irene McCray, who was financed by her high-rolling lover. Irene was well connected in the town, keeping the authorities at bay through bribes and social connections. She collaborated with a New Hampshire native, Charles B. Scrolls, who attempted to blockade Henry Wells and William G. Fargo, founders of Wells Fargo, from monopolizing the banking industry in San Francisco.

"Scrolls had his eye on the expansion of the railroad. He was determined to be the sole financier, but lacked sufficient assets until he was secretly informed of Uncle Bobby's prospecting success. So, Scrolls had hired some wranglers to do his dirty work. The brawl in the bar had been a ploy to give his men time to kill the guards and rob the wagons. He used the stolen gold to finance his business adventures."

"And he got away with it?" asked Matthew.

"Yep."

"How is that possible?"

"In those days, there was no one to stop him. The city had no mayor, no police force, and no system to investigate a robbery. Papa James was devastated, not only because he'd lost two million dollars' worth of gold, but because he realized the risks involved with prospecting. Uncle Bobby tried to convince Papa James to stay and continue mining, but there was no changing his mind. He gathered his portion of what remained of their wealth, returned home to Duwamp, and never prospected again. Instead, he shared his tales and all he knew about prospecting with his sons. Sadly, one of his sons, Uncle Jack, died of pneumonia, and Papa James never got over it. That same year, he was found dead in a tavern. But before he died, he taught his remaining son, Pop Angus, the six secrets of prospecting, which Pop would one day carry with him to Alaska, seeking his own fortune."

Alaska. My home—getting further away by the minute. The landscape outside had grown dark now, and the train hurtled forward into blackness. Uncle Joe and Matthew were quiet, and I was left alone with the gnawing hunger in my stomach and the ache of my grief and loss. Would I ever find my way back to the streams and forests, to the gold mines where I could fulfill my destiny?

3

Chicago

I'D BEEN IN CHICAGO FOR only ten minutes before I discovered something—I hated traffic. Before last week, I'd never even seen an automobile. Now there were hundreds, belching out nasty fumes as they roared up and down the dusty streets. I already despised everything about this city, and my anger intensified as we rode downtown in Uncle Joe's car.

Matthew did not share my feelings about automobiles. "Whoa," he exclaimed as he walked around the open-topped vehicle with black leather seats and royal blue paint on the body and tire rims.

Uncle Joe rested a hand on the hood, beaming with obvious pride. "She's a Cadillac. A Model G. First one just came out a year ago."

Matthew stopped in front of him. "One cylinder?"

Uncle Joe tapped the hood. "Four, actually. It's called Planetary Transmission Fours. And it's still got the counterclockwise cranking, although I was speaking to C. A. Black at a conference a few weeks back, and he says they're going to be changing both those things on the new models. He was pretty tightlipped about what they'd be changing them to, except to say the new models would revolutionize the automobile industry. Again."

Matthew walked around the car, shaking his head slowly back and forth. "How many horses?"

"Twenty-five, at least. Cadillac has always been conservative on their horsepower ratings, though."

I rolled my eyes and pushed past the two of them. Yanking open the back door of the car, I tossed my duffel bag onto the seat and gripped the metal on either side of the opening with both hands to pull myself up after it.

Uncle Joe pushed away from the car. "Laura's right. Time to go home."

Home seemed awfully far away at the moment. Everything was crowded here. People thronged down sidewalks lined with brick buildings built so close together there was barely room to walk between them. The streets were crammed with vehicles and things that looked like train cars but were attached to wires running above them. The words *The Chicago City Railway Company* were written across the side, so I guessed that's what they were: train cars designed to run along the street on tracks that were sunk down into the road.

It was impossible to look anywhere and see any open space, and a sudden homesickness gripped me. I'd been gone less than sixty-eight hours, and already I missed the mountains and fields and the river so much that I could hardly breathe. I crossed both arms across my chest and blinked rapidly, trying to hold back my tears and anger.

Matthew dropped onto the seat beside me and nudged me with his elbow. "You okay?"

I turned my head away.

We rode to Uncle Joe's in silence. I kept my eyes shut until the driver stopped the car, trying to summon up images of the forests and rivers of home. When I opened them, the view that greeted me caught me by surprise. I had no idea what Uncle Joe had done for a living since leaving prospecting, but he'd clearly found another way to strike gold.

A towering brick edifice rose up before us, set well back on a lush, green, perfectly manicured lawn. A low brick wall supported a six-foot-tall, black metal fence that circled the property, meeting in a pair of massive gates with the letter D embedded in the center of each one. Neatly trimmed shrubs lined the base of the fence down both sides of the property as far as I could see. As I watched, both gates swung open and the  driver eased the car slowly along the circular, brick-lined driveway and pulled up outside the large double front doors of the house.

Uncle Joe smacked his hands together, and I jumped. "Home sweet home, at last."

We followed Uncle Joe into the house, though "mansion" might be a more accurate term. Even Matthew whistled at the opulence surrounding us as we walked into the spacious foyer. The ceiling had to have been twenty feet above our heads. A chandelier hung above us, its hundreds of crystals capturing the sunlight from a high window and dropping shimmering splashes onto the walls and marble floor. A curving, wooden staircase rose up from the foyer to the floor above, and a balcony ran around all three sides of the second story, revealing more doors than I could count at first glance.

Two maids and a butler stood just inside the door. The maids wore short, black dresses with white aprons, and the butler a black suit and white tie. Matthew was in awe. I just scowled.

I did not know what Uncle Joe had done to become so rich, but whatever it was, he had a lot more money than the richest prospectors in Fairbanks. I was not ever going to admit to it, but I was impressed.

A woman came down the staircase, impeccably dressed, extending her hands in welcome. Uncle Joe kissed her, and then said, "Laura, Matthew, this is your Aunt Debra." I could see her surprise and confusion at my strange attire. Matthew politely shook her hand and said, "Pleased to meet you, ma'am." I said nothing. Uncle Joe whispered something to her, and she smiled warmly at me. "I'm sure you're both tired after the long journey. Ellie Mae will show you to your rooms." One of the maids stepped forward and gestured for us to follow. I picked up my duffel bag and stomped upstairs.

That night, I stayed in my bedroom, refusing to take a bath or eat dinner with them at the dining room table. The next day, I did the same, and the next. I also shunned the fancy clothes that soon lined the closet.

It wasn't long before Matthew was able to transfer to a local college to continue his education. He even got his own car. I had to attend a prestigious, all-girls private academy.

Every day after school, I went straight to my bedroom and did not come out until the next morning. I seldom spoke, not even to Matthew. Mr. Robinson, the head butler, always brought me a plate of food, but I didn't touch it until he closed the door behind him. I did toss my clothes to the head maid to wash; even I was repulsed by how dirty they were—thick with city grime.

I was bored, restless, and lonely. Day after day, alone in my room, I would review all the things Dad had taught me about safety and signs for a rockslide. For months, I was convinced that his death could not have been an accident. *Someone killed Dad to steal his spot for prospecting.*

Eventually, I let that go. I had to face the facts: that I would never know what really happened to Dad, or why he died. Nevertheless, my anger didn't subside. As crazy as it sounds, I was angry with him. *How could he do this? How could he leave me alone? Why didn't he see the loose rocks? Why did he mine in an area that was unsafe? Why? Why? WHY?*

* * * * *

Mr. Robinson drove me to school each morning in a black car called a limousine. The driver's seat was in the open air, but I was required to ride in the closed back compartment and was not permitted to roll down my windows. I hated it—I hated everything and everyone—and I was not afraid to let everyone know how I felt.

At school, I landed in the chancellor's office at least once a week. The other girls had made fun of me from day one, and my right hand and forearm were constantly cramping because each time I got into trouble, I had to write one hundred times: *I will follow the rules, respect authority, and learn to conform to society.*

Oh, the grief I gave Uncle Joe; I didn't care for him in any regard. Every time I thought of him, I'd feel my blood begin to boil. Why did he leave the family business? Why didn't he stay in contact with Dad? Did he think he was better than us? His fancy clothes, fancy cars, and fancy house were a slap in the face. Did he hate Dad or Pop Angus? Well, I hated him—and I also hated Aunt Debra with her fancy clothes, who wouldn't let me wear my waders in the house, and hired a "manners" instructor to come to the house to train me in etiquette and ethics for social activities and community events. I had no choice; I had to learn how to sit, to stand, when to speak and when not to speak. I was told what fork to use for a salad and which one was for the main course. Who cares?

Uncle Joe and Aunt Debra had no children, so I felt like they were trying to turn me into the daughter they never had. My first Christmas in Chicago, Aunt Debra took me to Marshall Fields, a posh new store, to purchase a dress, shoes, and accessories for a party Uncle Joe was throwing for his employees.

I could hear the music coming up the stairs as I got ready in my room. Every few minutes, the doorbell would ring and the soon the hum of conversation and bursts of laughter filled the house. Ellie Mae came and knocked on my door twice to inform me that Uncle Joe and Aunt Debra were waiting for me. Everyone else was downstairs, but I was stalling. I stood looking in the mirror, staring at the dress, dreading the moment I would have to leave my room. *I can't believe I'm doing this. Who is that girl in the mirror?* I remembered the man in Denver who had told me, "Be yourself." Yeah, right. I didn't even know this person looking back at me.

A third knock thundered on my bedroom door. "Ellie Mae," I yelled, "I told you the last time, I would be there when I get there."

"It's not Ellie Mae, Laura; it's me, Matthew."

"Knock on that door again, Matthew, and I will come out there and—"

"Everyone is here and Uncle Joe is about to make a toast and they are waiting for you. You need to hurry."

"Fine," I seethed. I hustled to the door and swung it open with great force, ready to punch Matthew, but before I could, he jumped back.

"What are you wearing?" he asked.

I paused for a second. "It's called a dress, Matthew, and if you say one more word, so help me—"

"No," he said, pointing toward the floor. "*What* are you wearing?"

Peeping out from under the ridiculous dress were my work boots, the same ones I wore when I chopped wood, hiked in the forest, or went hunting and fishing with Dad. They had seen their days of mud and rain and snow. The outside leather was tattered, worn, and ripped on the toes. But I loved them. They were mine. I had been about to take them off, reluctantly, and put on the fancy party shoes Aunt Debra had bought for me. But now I had a better idea. I was going to the party, boots and all.

Pushing past Matthew, I paraded down the eight-foot-wide spiral staircase, lined with deep red carpet, which descended into the formal living room.

"Here she is," Aunt Debra announced to everyone, her face lit up with pride and anticipation to see me in my finery.

Everyone turned. My long white gown puffed out around me, making it difficult to walk. Three steps into the room, I stepped on my dress and tumbled down, hitting the hardwood floor with a thud.

The women gasped.

"Are you all right?" Uncle Joe asked.

"I'm fine," I said as I dragged myself to my feet.

Once I regained my stance, I remembered my etiquette teacher's instructions. I gripped my dress on either side, lifted it slightly, gently bent my knees, and bowed my head in a curtsey before the dignitaries and special guests. As I did so, my work boots were exposed for all to see.

Gasps and murmurs filled the air. Ellie Mae smiled, then quickly dropped her head. Aunt Debra did not say a word—her look said it all.

"Mr. Robinson, hand Laura a glass so I can make a toast and get the festivities started," said Uncle Joe, his face unreadable.

I felt a certain satisfaction at ruffling the feathers of all those stuffy dignitaries and pampered ladies. I was being myself, just like the kind stranger at the diner had told me to.

* * * * *

Two years came and went. I wore out my beloved boots and had to succumb to wearing the shoes that Aunt Debra had bought me. I talked to her and Uncle Joe when spoken to, but I sure didn't start any conversations. I was coming to the end of my senior year in high school, and I couldn't wait for graduation so I'd finally be free to leave Chicago and return to Fairbanks. But how could I get there when I had no money? I begged Uncle Joe to send me back, but he only said, "You're not ready."

Not ready. How would he know? I was tough enough to survive on my own and make a living panning for gold. I'd been training for this since I was six years old. Uncle Joe had never spent as much time as I did in the river. What did he know about prospecting?

Instead, Uncle Joe promised to buy me a new car if I would go to college. At first, I refused. Why would I willingly go back to school? How ridiculous! Besides, Matthew thought it was a great idea, and for that reason alone, I wanted nothing to do with it. Nevertheless, after some persuasion, I agreed. The truth was, I wanted a car so I could make my escape.

Graduation came and went, and the long summer months stretched ahead of me—lonely and monotonous. Matthew and Uncle Joe were working every day, and Aunt Debra was always busy attending tea parties and community events, or shopping. She was kind and always invited me to go along, but that sounded like a fate worse than boredom to me.

One Friday morning, I decided to wander around the house and look for something to keep my mind occupied. I was anxious. I wanted to be left alone, but at the same time, I hated loneliness. I wandered into the kitchen, opened cabinets and drawers, and gazed at all the china, cups, saucers, pots, and pans.

I meandered down the hallways, stopping at each elaborately framed painting, noticing as if for the first time the intricate patterns of the wallpaper and the luxurious fabric of the drapes. As I peeked into different rooms, it seemed like every couch had twenty pillows. The windows were crystal clear, with not a single spot or cobweb showing.

I walked toward the den and heard Ellie Mae humming as she dusted. She looked up at me, startled, as I entered. "Miss Laura, you surprised me ... Can I get you anything?"

"How 'bout a beer?"

She laughed. "Now, Miss Laura, you know we don't keep alcohol in the manor." She knew I wasn't serious, but she'd never heard me crack a joke before, so she played along. "There's a pub on 24ᵗʰ Street. I can have Mr. Robinson drive you there."

"Maybe tomorrow," I answered as she continued to laugh. "Thanks anyway ... I'm fine." I was far away from being fine, but I didn't have anyone to blame. It was my choice to be miserable, even though everyone was trying to help me. I felt that if I let go of my anger and pain, I'd be forgetting my dad.

I just wanted to go back to Alaska. I wanted my dad back. I wanted my cabin back. I wanted to hear the river flow and the wind blow. I wanted to be dirty again—with fresh mountain dirt—and smell like sweat.

"Are you all right, Miss Laura?"

"Sure I am, Ellie Mae."

"It was good seeing you." She smiled.

You see me every day, but you don't see the real me. Then I realized what she meant. She meant that it was good to see me out of my room, something that had not happened more than five or six times in the past twenty-four months. Every day she delivered my breakfast and dinner to my room and returned to gather my tray. Ellie Mae was a sweetheart. It always amazed me how hard she worked. Short and stout, she was always energetic and never complained; she would do anything to make me happy.

I had had enough. My tour was over. The expansive rooms and long hallways made me feel trapped and desperate. The mansion was not my castle; I felt like a prisoner.

I stood there, closed my eyes, and tried to remember what freedom felt like—the winding forest trails where I rode on Stud, my mule; the ever-changing river with its endless promise of riches; the night sky lit up by hundreds of thousands of stars, unmarred by city lights. I focused on the sound of the water rushing by. I could hear Dad call my name when he found a spot for us to pan. I felt his hand in mine as we walked through the woods late in the evening after a long day at work. During the cold winters, I would fall behind and step into his footprints when the snow was too deep for me. Memories were all I had now.

"Miss Laura, where are you?" Ellie Mae asked.

I turned and stumbled out of the room. I didn't want to even think about where I was.

4

The Office

I HAD NEVER BEEN IN this hallway before. The sound of Ellie Mae's humming receded into silence as I made my way to the door at the end. From Matthew's descriptions, I deduced that this must be Uncle Joe's office, or "library," as he called it. *Who has a library in their house?* Matthew told me he'd spent many evenings in there with Uncle Joe. Curiosity got the best of me. *Why not?* As I reached for the doorknob, I noticed a sign fastened on the door. *Know What You're Looking For.*

Was it a riddle or some type of warning to stay out? *Well, if Matthew can go in, I can too.*

I reached down and grasped the decorative door handle, turning it slowly, as if I were breaking into a bank. As I pushed the door open, my heart raced. I stepped inside quickly and closed the door behind me. *So, this is it.* The room was massive, and its back wall was lined with shelves from floor to ceiling. Pictures, awards, trophies and plaques adorned the other three walls.

Who are you, Uncle Joe?

In the middle of the room was a large, handmade oak desk with decorative carvings on each corner. A high-backed leather couch faced the desk, with two chairs on each side. The plush brown carpet appeared to be three inches thick. I made my way around the room, looking at the pictures. In the first, two men stood beside one another shaking hands. Attached to the bottom frame was a metal plaque with the words: "Fred A. Busse, Chicago Mayor, 1907." To the left was a picture of Uncle Joe and a man with a thick mustache and a bow tie. The description read: "John R. Tanner, Governor of Illinois, 1901."

Each picture seemed to show Uncle Joe with one dignitary or another. One featured Uncle Joe with a baseball player, the stadium in the background. This one had a handwritten signature, "Billy Sullivan." The caption below read: "To Joseph Dunagan from the Chicago White Sox, World Series Champions, 1906, Billy Sullivan." *Matthew must have loved that*, I thought. I didn't know anything about baseball, but he was an avid fan. As I continued around the room, many of the names were unfamiliar, although I had the uneasy sense that I should have known who these people were. Edgar Rice Burroughs. Ernest Hemingway. Carl Sandburg. Marshall Field. George Pullman. Then one picture in particular made me catch my breath. It was Uncle Joe and John D. Rockefeller. Even I knew that name. *Wow, Uncle Joe, you're famous!*

Next was a picture of Uncle Joe and a man with a full, white beard and mustache, like Santa Claus. The caption read, "Andrew Carnegie." Carnegie ... why did I know that name? And then, there he was, in the next picture—the man I had met in the railroad diner in Denver. Dale Carnegie.

I turned to the next wall, and the pictures there captured my attention much more than those of all the famous people. Alaska! There were photographs of bearded men standing in the river panning for gold, wearing waders and brimmed hats, holding picks and pans. One by one I studied these images, but none had a caption on the frame. I was mesmerized. I'd had no idea that Uncle Joe had such a connection to the life he'd left behind.

Just then, I saw a box on the floor in the corner of the room. It looked out of place because everything else was so neatly organized. I leaned down to read the description on the box: "Billy Dunagan." *Wait a minute ... that's Dad!* The box was secured with string, but I was able to move it enough to peek inside. There were stacks of letters addressed to Dad—dozens and dozens of letters, but all of them were unopened. *Why does Uncle Joe have Dad's mail?* I wanted to know more, but I couldn't take the letters out without breaking the string. I pushed the string back into place and straightened the lid to its original form.

This office was becoming a mystery, and I wanted to figure out just who Joseph Dunagan was. Near the desk was a round table, upholstered with coffee-brown textured leather and black rivets, and edged with gold. I moved toward it.

Then I saw them.

Prospecting tools? Displayed like a museum exhibit, in a glass case atop the table, were an oval prospecting pan, a pick, and a small hammer, just like Dad and I had used in the river. And beside them was an old, worn, hand-bound leather notebook. I looked closer to read the title written on the front of the book: *The Greatest Prospector In The World.*

"Holy smoke!" I said aloud. I wanted to investigate further, but the glass case was fastened to the table. As I stood there staring at the book, the pick, the hammer, and the prospecting pan, all my pain, sorrow, and loneliness returned. I closed my eyes, remembering the river as tears pooled in them. *I can't do this ... I can't lose it right now! Get it together, Laura!*

Fighting back the tears, I opened my eyes. On the wall in front of me, above the round table, was a picture I hadn't noticed before, of three men in prospecting clothes, posing in waders. When I looked closer, I recognized the man on the right, who was squatting down. Dad! To the left, I identified a younger Uncle Joe, and behind him was none other than Pop Angus. Several more pictures showed Dad and Uncle Joe, and there was even a picture of Dad and me at the river. I wondered for a moment how on earth Uncle Joe got that, but then I remembered when our neighbor Mrs. Oliver got a new camera and insisted on taking our picture.

I looked back at the photo of Dad, Uncle Joe, and Pop Angus. They looked so happy and relaxed there in the river, doing what they'd been born to do. Carefully, I reached up and removed it from the wall, held it in my hands, and stared into Dad's eyes, wishing he were here.

* * * * *

Suddenly, I heard the doorknob turn. I had no idea how long I had been standing there. I fumbled to replace the picture on the wall before the door opened, but before I could mount it back in position, the door swung open. Quickly, I slung my hand behind my back, gripping the picture as tightly as I could.

There stood Uncle Joe.

My heart sank. I felt like a criminal being served a warrant for arrest.

"Uncle Joe, I'm sorry for coming in here without your permission ... I'll go back to my room." I placed the picture on the edge of the oval table and started toward the door, hoping to miss out on the inevitable lecture or reprimand.

"Hold on, hold on." Uncle Joe held up both his hands.

I was not in the mood to be confronted and questioned. I paused and lowered my head. "I'm sorry, Uncle Joe. I'm really sorry. It won't happen again."

"Sorry? You don't need to be sorry. You can come in here any time."

His words startled me. I lifted my head and looked up at him. I wanted to leave, but I felt trapped, embarrassed and not sure how to respond. *Why did I leave my room?*

An awkward silence filled the room. I waited for him to say something, but he just stood there smiling. "Can I go now?"

"I think it's about time we have a talk, Laura."

I would almost have preferred him to be angry. At least confrontations were something I was used to. I wanted to run back to my bedroom and hide. But this time, I could not.

Uncle Joe pointed to the couch. "Please, take a seat."

I sat down at the far end.

He picked up the picture I had removed from the wall, then sat in the chair nearest to me.

"Laura, I've been wanting to talk to you for some time now, but I knew that I had to wait for the right time."

I took a deep breath, then exhaled slowly. "Okay."

"I know how mad you've been, and how hard it was for you to leave Alaska." Uncle Joe's voice was soft and low. "I want you to know that I never intended to hurt you or cause you any discomfort. These two years have been the most difficult of your life, and I believe I can help you, if you will allow me to explain."

I really didn't know what to say other than, "Okay," again.

He placed the picture on his desk, sat back in his chair, crossed his legs, and started twisting his mustache. "Let's start at the beginning."

"As you already know, my grandfather, Papa James, was the first prospector in our family. His adventures in San Francisco had both a positive and a negative effect upon him. Some people, looking at his life, would say he failed because he never returned to prospecting.

"Truth is, he learned more about life than he did about gold. He shared his experiences and valuable life lessons with his son, Pop Angus—my father and your grandfather.

"Like Papa James, Pop Angus despised anyone who cheated, lied, or promoted things that would destroy a family, such as alcohol, gambling, or lewd and unbecoming behavior. Pop taught your father and me to have integrity and work smart as well.

"When Pop fell on hard times and lost his investments, he didn't mope, complain, or grumble. Instead, he looked for an opportunity of advancement. When news spread of gold in Alaska, and Pop decided to move, I did not want to leave Seattle. I wanted to stay, but I felt like Pop needed my support.

"When we started prospecting, we struggled at first, but Pop had a plan to get us through. Every day but Sunday, we went to the river and panned for gold. It was exciting, and oh, what a thrill it was when we found gold. Those were some of the best days of my life."

I leaned forward, captivated despite myself, at hearing Uncle Joe's side of the family history.

"Like yours, my mom also died when I was young, and Pop did the best he could to raise your dad and me with dignity and honor. Pop was a hard worker and a brilliant businessman who was full of wisdom. He knew what it took to succeed, and he believed that you could become whatever you wanted to be in life, if you applied certain principles for success."

Uncle Joe paused for a moment, remembering.

"After we spent the first couple of months panning for gold, Pop had a talk with your dad and me. He told us that prospecting for gold was exciting, but there were other ways in life to prosper. Hundreds of people were following the Klondike dream. Sure, I loved it, but at the time, there were no regulations for land, and people were killed every day, fighting over territories and locations for gold. Theft, murder, robberies, and scandals were more prevalent then than at any other time in Alaska and California. It was just part of life back then.

"But Pop wanted more for us. He shared what Papa James gained from his experiences with prospecting, and told us that if we would follow six secrets, we would succeed in life. And then Pop insisted that your dad and I move to Chicago."

My jaw dropped. I could not believe what he was saying!

"It's true, Laura. I promise. That is how it happened. Pop sat your dad and me down and begged us to leave Alaska and head for Chicago. We both said no. We loved prospecting for gold, and we would never leave him. But he insisted that we follow his advice. As hard as it was—and it broke my heart—I submitted to my father's wishes. I left Alaska for Chicago to get an education and move on with my life.

"Billy was stubborn—that's where you get it from, Laura. He refused to go. And when your dad got something in his mind, he was not going to change. Before I left, Pop asked me to try and convince him to leave with me. We got into a big argument that night, and he told me to leave and never come back.

"I loved him and it broke my heart that he got so mad at me. I tried to talk to him again, before I left Sitka, but your dad would not speak with me, nor would he change his mind. I have had to live with that night my entire life. The last words your father said to me were, 'You're dead to me.' It broke my heart."

I couldn't quite take it in. The picture he was painting was so different from what I had always thought—and he was different too. I slumped in my corner of the couch while he readjusted his position.

"After Matthew was born, I came to Dawson City, but your dad had already moved to Fairbanks. I went there to see him, but he refused to let me into the cabin, the one where you were raised. That is when I met Mrs. Oliver, your neighbor. We had a meal together, and I told her my story, then asked if she would send telegrams keeping me updated on my brother's life.

"She did just that. I came to visit a second time, shortly after you were born, but once again, your father refused to allow me into the cabin. My final visit was after your mom died. I did not get there in time for the funeral, so I went to Mrs. Oliver's home, and you and Matthew were there. She was caring for you two while your dad was mining for gold. I left some money with Mrs. Oliver and asked her to buy you both whatever she deemed necessary."

I tried to remember meeting Uncle Joe, but I had been too young. No one ever told me that he came to visit us, not even Mrs. Oliver.

"That was the last time I went to Alaska, until your dad—" He stopped, words seeming to catch in this throat, and put his head in his hands.

I did not know what to say. Along with being shocked, I was mad all over again, but for a different reason now. I heard Uncle Joe sniffle as he lifted his head. He was crying real tears. I had never seen a man cry.

"I loved Billy ... your dad ... with all my heart," Uncle Joe said, wiping the tears from his face. "I wrote him so many letters, but he never responded. Before I left the cottage, I searched your dad's room and found all my letters, unopened."

That explained the box in the corner.

"Does Matthew know all this?"

"Every bit," he replied.

As I sat back in my chair, fresh anger welled up inside me. *Matthew knew this the whole time, but he never said a word. I'm going to kill him.*

"Now, don't you be mad at your brother. He wanted to tell you, but I forbade him. I wanted to be the one to explain things to you, but I knew you were not ready. If I had told you too soon, you would have overreacted, rejected the truth, and run away."

I had to admit he was right. That is exactly how I would have responded.

"There is so much more I want to tell you, but I think it is best if you let this information sink in, and that we talk more at another time. Would you like that?" Uncle Joe asked.

I wanted to ask him about the book in the glass case, but I needed to digest the revelations of the past hour. I wasn't sure I could take in much more right then.

"Can I go now?"

"Sure you can. But before you do, I want you to know how much your dad loved you. Don't let anger or bitterness overtake you, now that you know the truth about what separated your father and me. Your dad made his decision, and he did his best. What's most important is where we go from here."

I got up from the couch and walked toward the door. "Laura?"

I turned, folding my arms across my chest. "Yes?"

"Dinner is at six. I would like to invite you to eat with us at the table tonight ... if you're up for it."

I paused. I really did not want to say yes. But I was too confused to know how to respond. "I'll think about it."

How could I even consider joining them for dinner when I couldn't even think straight?

* * * * *

Back in my room, I contemplated what to do. It was 5:45 p.m., and I felt as if I were making the greatest decision of my life. I watched the clock on the wall. Each minute that passed meant dinnertime was closer, and my anxiety peaked. *I can't do it.* The one person I thought I could trust had let me down. Was everything he had taught me just a lie? *Not tonight.*

At ten minutes past six, Ellie Mae brought my dinner: roasted chicken, green beans, mashed potatoes and homemade rolls. I sat there on my bed with the tray of food on my lap, lost in my memories and questions. An hour went by before I heard a knock on the door. "Miss Laura, can I take your tray?"

A few moments later, Ellie Mae opened the door, then quickly slipped in and out, taking the tray with her. She seemed to know I didn't want to talk.

I decided I was not going back to Uncle Joe's office—ever. My pain was too great. But I kept thinking about the Alaskan pictures that covered the wall; the oval table with the prospecting tools; the picture of Dad, Uncle Joe, and Pop Angus above the table; and *that* book—*The Greatest Prospector In The World.*

Across the room were my overalls and waders, Dad's hat, and my army green bag with Dad's prospecting tools. I had intentionally placed them on the stand so that I would never forget the river, Alaska, or my dad. For two years, they had been my source of motivation to get out of Chicago. Now, as I stared at them, I felt empty.

I lifted myself off the bed, sighing, and shuffled over to the stand. I gathered up my memorabilia, opened the door to my closet, and put everything in the trunk. I wanted to forget.

5

Rejected

I STARTED SCHOOL THAT FALL at the University of Illinois, and true to his word Uncle Joe bought me a car: a 1910 Premier Two Door Touring car. It arrived from Indianapolis two days before the semester began. It had wooden spokes, cream paint, and a black canvas top with red leather bucket seats. Initially, I thought he bought it because he felt sorry for me. *He said I was ready—yeah right, ready to punch someone or something.*

Uncle Joe had wanted me to live on campus, but I was not ready to be around people yet. I still spent every day in my bedroom. Once the semester began, Matthew, who was still attending the same school, drove me crazy. He wanted to walk me to each class, study with me, and help me with my homework. I knew he had good intentions and truly cared about me, but I just wanted him to shut up and leave me alone.

Since that conversation in Uncle Joe's office, I had stopped thinking about Alaska. I even forgot about the book in the glass case. Somehow, I blocked out everything that had mattered so much to me. I just focused on my studies, staying in my room and wondering what would become of my life.

* * * * *

I managed to graduate from the University of Illinois in June 1916, with a degree in business. There had been very few other girls in my classes, but I didn't care. I'd wanted a degree that would actually be useful. My relationship with Uncle Joe had developed during my college years. He was so supportive and encouraging, telling me that he always believed in me whenever he had the opportunity. I was still reclusive, but eventually I came to eat dinner at the table, for the most part.

Now that college life had ended, it was time to formulate a résumé. It wasn't much of one; I had not worked a single day while attending college. But I needed to find a job.

After six weeks of putting in applications and having interviews, I responded to an ad in the *Chicago Tribune* for a bookkeeper with Chicago Mercantile. After two interviews, I was ready to start work.

The job atmosphere was intense and fast-paced. Many nights, I had to sleep in the office, if I slept at all, just to keep up. Balancing books was the easy part. Dealing with people and their personalities was another thing. At first, I kept to myself and seldom talked. One of my co-workers nicknamed me "Mouse" because he said I was quiet as a church mouse.

Even though I still felt lost, I met new people and started to believe something good was coming. I could see hope on the horizon, and I wondered where life was taking me. And then, without warning, I was fired. After just three months!

Stunned, I demanded an explanation, but my supervisor told me to go home. I would not take no for an answer. I returned the next day and asked for a meeting with the chief financial officer. The secretary scheduled an appointment for 9 a.m. the next day. I showed up at 8:45 a.m. but was

ignored in the waiting room until 3 p.m. With the workday coming to a close, I decided that I had had enough; I stomped up to the secretary's desk. "Why have I waited all day for my scheduled appointment?"

She glanced up at me, then pulled out her calendar book, seeming flustered. "Well, the CFO has been out of the office all day."

I was furious. Did she think I had time to waste? "I'll be back tomorrow, and every day, until I can see him, do you understand?" Before she could answer, I stormed out of the office.

I returned to my former workplace every day for nine days straight, until I finally was able to meet with the CFO. I spent thirty seconds with him before being told that I was an unexpected casualty of the Great War.

Everyone knew that the economy was struggling because of the war in Europe. When I walked into the beauty salon the next day, I discovered that three other women had been fired from their jobs, and each one had been told that it was because of the war. I thought it was a lame excuse and was convinced I'd been terminated because I was a woman.

Those nine days trying to meet with the CFO allowed me to delay explaining to anyone, especially Uncle Joe, what had happened. It also gave me time to find another job. Sam, an accountant at Chicago Mercantile, had a cousin who was employed at the *Chicago Tribune*. He gave me his name and phone number, and told me to tell his cousin that Sam had sent me. I knew he had a crush on me, because he often brought coffee and doughnuts to my office, and twice he asked me to have lunch with him. I was kind, but always had an excuse as to why I could not.

Sam's cousin put in a good word, and I got a job as an assistant in the advertising department. After I was hired, I told Uncle Joe about what had happened, and explained that I was now working at the *Chicago Tribune*. Uncle Joe knew Joseph Patterson, the associate editor, but he never told him that I was his niece, or used his friendship to get me any personal favors or promotions. Uncle Joe was odd like that.

By my second week of working at the *Tribune*, I started making friends with a few other girls my age. Unless we had a deadline to meet, we had lunch every day at a nearby restaurant. Many nights after work, some of us girls would go out to eat, recapping our workday and gossiping about our bosses. Over the next two years, we built strong bonds of friendship that would later develop into great business relationships.

One of my co-workers, Sandy, who worked in payroll, was from Seattle. She had lived there until she was fourteen. She told me how she had struggled when moving away from her friends. At first, she did not like Chicago, and it took her some time to adjust. I felt she was genuine, and I told her bits and pieces about my life in Alaska.

In November 1918, the Great War in Europe ended, but we in Chicago hardly noticed. The city was busy fighting its own war against a terrible influenza epidemic. Large gatherings were banned, schools were shut down, theaters and cabarets were closed, and children were not allowed to play in the city parks. Even the church services were cut short. Businesses worked in shifts to avoid overcrowding. We wore gauze masks, and public spitting was outlawed. People were encouraged to walk to work rather than crowd into the streetcars, where the risk of infection was high. I was grateful to have my own car as I watched people trudging to the office during the frigid mornings. More people died of the disease that winter than had died during all four years of the war. Eight thousand five hundred people died in Chicago alone, including the former mayor.

* * * * *

After two years of hard work, I was promoted to personal assistant for the new associate editor, Robert McCormick, who was Mr. Patterson's cousin. Soon after that, a power struggle developed between Mr. McCormick and Mr. Patterson. They had conflicting views as to the direction of the newspaper, including politics, the military, the war, and other issues. The feud became vicious, and the employees were forced to choose sides. To me, it was childish. Manipulation and intimidation were daily obstacles, and I was tired of the theatrics. One day, I voiced my opinion to Mr. McCormick.

He stood for almost a minute in enraged silence, his face turning red with fury. When he finally calmed down enough to speak, he simply said, "How dare you come into my office and give me your views. You're just a woman ... Get out!"

The following day, I was called into Human Resources and told I was no longer Mr. McCormick's assistant. I was now to work as an editor in the sports department.

I smiled as I took the elevator down to the third floor. This could almost be seen as a promotion; I would be doing my own work, not responding to the whims of a power-hungry bully. But when I arrived on the third floor, I could not believe my eyes. There were only two small offices, one for the chief editor and one for the head writer. Everyone else worked in cubicles that were divided by a maze of half walls, which took up the entire room. The noise and commotion—telephones ringing, typewriters crashing, multiple voices shouting at once—filled the space, along with an oppressive cloud of cigarette smoke choking the air. I felt like I had walked into hell itself!

I was the only woman in the department, and the men acted as if they had never seen one before. After I introduced myself to the chief editor, he assigned me a cubicle. As I walked toward my new workspace, men started whistling and howling like dogs, tossing out rude comments like a pack of drunken sailors.

"Hey, baby," said a rugged unshaven man with his cigarette hanging from his lips, as I walked by.

Some made obscene hand gestures, while others puckered up their lips, as if wanting a kiss. I had almost reached my cubicle when a man stepped out and blocked my path. "Well, look what we got here—Mary Pickford in the flesh." I knew

Mary Pickford was a famous, attractive actress who had a slim build and long curly hair, similar to the way I wore mine.

I stopped and waited for him to move, one hand on my hip. After a moment, I got tired of waiting. When I tried to walk around him to the left, he shifted his position. So I moved to the right, but he moved in front of me.

"Sir, I recommend that you move out of my way and let me pass."

"Ya think so, little lady?" he sneered.

A group of men now gathered around, laughing.

The man stood his ground. "And what if I don't?" he replied, challenging me. The smirk on his face ticked me off.

"Look, I don't want any trouble." I felt like I was back in the schoolyard facing a bully. "So I'm going to ask you politely one more time—get the heck out of my way!"

Now the gathered men laughed and cheered and applauded my boldness.

The man unbuttoned his sports jacket and placed his hands on his hips. "We got a feisty one here, boys!"

I wasn't going to let this bully stand in the way of my new job. "I'll tell you what. I'm going to count to three, and if you haven't moved out of my way, I will not ask nicely again."

I counted "one" and he did not move. "Two," and he just grinned. So as the number "three" passed my lips, I kicked the man hard in the crotch. He dropped like a rockslide, hands clutched between his legs. I stepped around him, made my way to my cubicle, and sat down at the small desk. All the men laughed and cheered for me, as if I had just dropped heavyweight champion Jack Dempsey in the first round. Despite myself, I felt a smile sliding across my face. This might be a fun job after all.

Even so, after my glory faded, I felt fear set in. As I sat at my desk, my heart pounded to the point I thought I would pass out. I took a deep breath, closed my eyes, and gathered my thoughts, wondering what the man would do once he regained his composure. It seemed strange, but he did not retaliate. In fact, I gained the respect of all the men, and no one harassed me again.

I tried to continue eating lunch with Sandy and the girls from the tenth floor, but it was not the same. I had lost my place of honor. I'd been ostracized from the inner circle and only Sandy would talk to me.

* * * * *

Three weeks went by after my victorious entry into the sports department, and I was doing my best. But I was not trained to be an editor; I was a bookkeeper. I continued to make mistakes that went into print. After my third printed error, I landed in the Human Resources office again. This time, they demoted me to distribution and circulation, where the newspapers were loaded onto trucks. I knew they did this to make me quit. The fact that I wore a "flapper" dress to work—women didn't wear pants in public in the early 1900s—also riled my boss. But how was I supposed to load trucks in a full-length dress and a corset? Would they have preferred me to wear my bib overalls?

On my third day, the newspapers included a special edition. This made the paper stacks, wrapped in bundles of fifty, so heavy that I struggled to lift them. Sure enough, I dropped a stack of papers off the truck onto the cement floor.

My supervisor had watched it happen and marched right over to me. "What is wrong with you? If you weren't such a weak, silly woman, that wouldn't have happened." He was pushing; he wanted to get a reaction from me.

So I gave him one: I cussed him out. I shouldn't have, but my anger got the best of me.

He smiled triumphantly, as if he had won some grand victory. "Get out of here—you're fired!"

When I attempted to defend my actions, he just turned around and walked away.

It was only 7:30 a.m., and I didn't want to go home that early. So I drove around the city for the next three hours. I could not believe this was happening to me! I'd been at the *Tribune* for over two years. I'd made new friends and was starting to feel that life might be something other than misery and boredom.

In my desperation and anger, I started thinking about Alaska for the first time in several years. What would my life have been like now, had I never come to Chicago? What if Dad were still alive, and I had finished school and was working with him full-time, panning for gold?

As I reminisced, I cried—something I had not done for almost six years. *What's wrong with me?* I pondered my thoughts while waiting for the traffic signal to change. I was frustrated with life, embarrassed that I'd been fired again, and dreading what Matthew might say.

As nightfall came, I snuck into Uncle Joe's house and up the stairs without anyone seeing me. I quickly changed into my nightclothes and climbed under the covers.

I stayed in my room for three days, refusing to eat or talk to anyone. Replaying the scenario of my dismissal over and over again, I just felt more and more angry and bitter.

One evening, I heard a knock on my door.

"Miss Laura, if you don't eat something, I'm going to tell Mr. Joe. I've covered for you long enough."

Ellie Mae entered, with a tray of dinner. The smell of roast chicken wafted over me, and for the first time in days, I actually felt hungry. I sighed deeply. "Okay, I'll eat whatever you brought."

Her sweet smile melted my resistance. I couldn't face that smile, not yet.

I pulled the covers over my head. "Why is my life so awful?"

"Now, Miss Laura, your life isn't so bad. You're just going through some things. You'll come out of it. You'll see."

I could hear her smile; the covers weren't helping. "I don't belong here."

"Where do you belong, Miss Laura?"

"I don't know ... maybe Alaska." The smell of roast chicken was also finding its way through the covers. Admitting defeat, I sat up and took the tray.

"But you aren't in Alaska, girl. You're in Chicago now." She paused, then added, "Maybe someday you can go back there, but for now you're here. And once you realize that, get up and move on, you can dream again. I believe in you, Miss Laura. You can be anything you want to be if you just believe."

I did not know what to say. I was not in a believing mood. "Do you have anything that will help me sleep?"

"My momma always gave us warm milk," Ellie Mae replied.

"Did it work?" It sounded awful.

"It sure does. You eat up your dinner and I'll fetch you some right now." When she returned about five minutes later with a cup of warm milk, I drank it and lay back on my pillow.

Ellie Mae sat down on the bed and tucked me in as if I were a little girl. "I'll say a prayer for you." She combed my hair away from my eyes with her finger. "Now, you rest, Miss Laura." She turned off the lamp beside my bed, picked up the empty mug, and walked toward my bedroom door.

"I will." I rolled over and curled up into a ball, ready to sleep my sadness away. I'm not sure if it was the milk, Ellie Mae's tenderness, or the fact that I was so exhausted, but I was soon sound asleep.

6

The Dream

THAT NIGHT, I DREAMED I was back home, standing in the rushing water in Fairbanks, Alaska. I instantly recognized the place. It was one that Dad had discovered when I was ten, and we had visited it many times over a two-year period. It was one of my favorite spots, not only because we found gold there, but because it was a place Dad had taught me several panning techniques. And best of all, it was a place where we would sit on the bank, eating lunch and laughing, as he told me stories about Pop Angus and Papa James.

It had been more than a decade since I'd seen that place, but suddenly, now, I was back there. I was in midstream, holding my prospecting pan in my hand, the cold, crisp water beating against my thighs, chilling them even through my waders.

I could hear the river rushing by, see the trees, tall and lean, and feel the wind blowing against my face.

Suddenly, I heard my dad's voice. "Hey, you gonna pan, or ya getting tired?"

I spun around, and there he was, standing in the river in his waders, shaking his pan, smiling from ear to ear.

I grinned back, "I'm never tired!"

He laughed. "Well, how 'bout a break? You up for that?"

"Sure am." And for some reason I was, though I hadn't been a moment before.

We waddled our way out of the water to our favorite spot on the bank. Dad had carved several tree stumps into seats, with a back and arms on each side. A fire of hot coals heated up the coffee in a cast-iron pot. We warmed our hands and bellies as we sipped the hot black coffee together.

"How is it?" Dad asked.

"Black." We both laughed. That's what Dad had always said whenever someone asked him about his coffee.

Dad took another sip, adjusted his hat, and cleared his throat. "Laura, there's something I need to tell you."

His serious voice reminded me of the tone he used when he found out that I had been in a fight at school or sassed a teacher. My heart started pounding, and I reflected upon recent events, trying to figure out what I had done or hidden from him. I could not recall anything. "What's wrong, Dad?"

He took my hand in his. "Nothing is wrong, Laura. I'm just proud of you." He choked up, then cleared his throat again. "Getting your university degree is a great accomplishment."

Suddenly, my mind landed back in the present, the time in the dream racing to meet with reality. When I looked down at my hand, it was no longer the dirty-nailed, calloused hand of my twelve-year-old self, but my neatly manicured adult hand. I was confused for a moment, but then Dad reached out and took my coffee cup, setting it aside. He clasped both of my hands in his. "Laura, it's important that you remain in Chicago."

Now, I was fully aware that this was a dream, although I was still in it. I was no longer a child prospecting for gold in Alaska. My dad was not alive. *This is not real.* But I so wanted it to be real!

I leaped from my stump-chair and embraced my dad. He wrapped his arms around me and held me tight as I began to cry. "Dad, don't go, don't leave me ... not again!"

"It will be all right, baby." His voice was barely a whisper above the babble of the river and the wind in the trees.

"But it's not all right," I cried aloud.

"I'm with you every day," he said.

"Not like this, you're not," I protested.

"I know, sweetie, I know ... but I'm here now, and I want you to remember what I taught you about turning the bad into good."

"I've tried, Dad, but nothing goes my way!"

"I know about you getting fired from the *Chicago Tribune.*"

"Dad, I'm sorry I kicked that man, but he had it coming."

Dad started to laugh. "You dropped him, all right."

A smile broke through my tears.

"I know you liked that job, and you made friends there too."

"Yeah," I said. "I miss Sandy." In some ways, it seemed weird talking to Dad about my life in Chicago. And yet it came so effortlessly. He was always so easy to talk with, late at night, sitting around the potbelly stove.

"Don't worry," he said. "Those relationships you built there at the *Tribune* will endure, you'll see. That's why it's always important to build strong relationships, even if you don't know how they will benefit you in the future. Do you remember how I would build relationships with all the folks in town?"

"Yes, sir, I remember," I answered. Dad had been well liked and respected by almost everyone in the community where we lived, which was no small feat in the competitive and cut-throat world of prospecting.

"The men at the *Tribune*, those who fought for control, don't understand the value of relationships. They are not out to help others, only themselves. Those types of people are selfish, self-centered, egotistical, and full of greed. They will never teach you anything but how to walk all over people to get what you want. In the long run, they will die lonely deaths, with full bank accounts and hearts just as full of regret."

"Mr. McCormick was a nasty old coot who drank too much," I said with a grin.

"Everything flows from the top down. What is in a man will come out, and those who are under his leadership will either become just like him or grow bitter in the process. Life is too short to waste around people like him, Laura." He smiled and let go of my hands, picking up his coffee cup. "If you had remained at that job, it would have destroyed you. So it's not so bad that you got fired. There's no reason for you to fret, my pet; it will get better."

"I love it when you say that," I grinned.

"Say what?" he asked, as if he did not know. He just wanted to hear me say it.

"Don't fret, my pet," I answered.

He smiled, but then his face turned serious again. "Have you forgotten who you are? You always told me that someday, when you grew up, you would become the greatest prospector in the world.

"Daddy, you're the greatest prospector—not me," I replied.

"Baby girl, you're special. Something great is about to happen to you."

"I wish that were true, Daddy. I just want to stay here with you."

"I am with you, sweetie. Everything I taught you is inside you, but there's more that you need to learn to become the greatest prospector. Uncle Joe can help you."

"Uncle Joe?" I responded.

"Yes, Uncle Joe," he replied.

I am not sure why, but at the time, I did not seem to remember my conversation with Uncle Joe in the office. I suppose that is the way of dreams.

"How can he help me?" I asked.

"He can teach you the six secrets to prospecting," he replied. "Papa James and Uncle Bobby learned a lot about prospecting in their short time together. Papa shared his insights with Pop Angus. Pop was a smart man, much more so than people gave him credit for. Everyone loved him. He resolved more conflicts by following the principles Papa James passed down to him than any other man I ever knew.

"Pop Angus wrote down what his father taught him. When Uncle Joe left for Chicago, Pop gave him a book that he had written called *The Greatest Prospector In The World*. That book contains the six secrets to prospecting, and you need to ask him to teach them to you."

I was confused. How could Uncle Joe teach me about panning for gold, and what good would it do me to learn it, if I were to stay in Chicago? Hadn't Dad just told me that's what he wanted me to do?

He seemed to hear my questions even though I hadn't spoken aloud.

"Prospecting is a way of life; it's not just about gold," he said. "It is the secret to success, and it will bring you fulfillment. When you invest in others, building up people by helping them to discover their dreams, accomplish their goals, and reach their destinies, that is the greatest reward."

"But, Dad," I interrupted. "Uncle Joe has never asked me to learn from him."

"And he never will," he said. "You've got to want it. The protégé seeks the mentor, not the other way around. You have to be hungry, humble, and willing to learn. He cannot do that for you; only you can. And when you're ready, you will submit to him. So I'm telling you that it is time for you to seek out your mentor. Uncle Joe will teach you the secrets to prospecting. I cannot."

When he said, "I cannot," I started to cry again.

"Laura, you can do it," he insisted.

I threw my arms around him, holding him tight. "I won't let you go! I don't want you to leave me!" What if this were to be the last conversation I would ever have with him?

But Dad knew what was best. I had to move on. I had to let go of the past.

"I'll never let you go, pumpkin," he declared. He only called me pumpkin when I was "down in the dumps."

I squeezed my eyes shut, trying to hold on to the dream.

"Laura. Laura! LAURA! Wake up!"

I opened my eyes, peeking over the pillow that covered a portion of my face to see Ellie Mae sitting on the bed next to me. Then I closed my eyes again, wrapping my arms around my pillow as I mumbled, "Daddy, don't leave!"

Ellie Mae was shaking me. "Wake up, sleepy head. It's already 10:30 in the morning."

"He's gone, Ellie Mae," I said.

"Who's gone, Miss Laura?" she asked.

"My daddy," I replied.

"Yes, he is, pumpkin, and I'm sorry for your loss."

"You called me pumpkin!" I said, surprised.

She paused for a second. "I guess I did."

I started sobbing again. "You've never called me pumpkin before."

"Well, if it's gonna make you cry like that, I won't call you that again," she declared.

"No, no—it's a happy crying," I explained, wiping the tears from my eyes.

"In that case, I'll say it again: Pumpkin. Pumpkin. PUMPKIN!"

We both started laughing aloud.

Still chuckling, she said, "I guess that warm milk worked."

"I imagine it did," I replied, and laughed even more.

"Well, Mr. Joe and your brother have left for the day, and you missed breakfast. So why don't you gather yourself together, come downstairs to the kitchen, and let me cook you something special for lunch? Anything you want."

I remembered something my dad always made me on days when I was feeling down. "How about grilled cheese and tomato soup?"

"All right then, one grilled cheese sandwich and tomato soup, coming right up!" Ellie Mae ruffled my hair affectionately and left the room.

I still had my pillow clutched in my arms. Gently, I released my grip, looked up at the ceiling and said, "I love you, Daddy." The tears flowed again, but this time they did not seem to hurt. Something had changed, and I felt different, somehow free.

* * * * *

I could smell the aroma of grilled cheese from the other side of the house.

"That smells good," I said as I entered the kitchen.

Ellie Mae turned around and said, "Sure it does; it's my secret recipe." We both laughed; it was just bread and cheese.

As I tucked in, I shared bits and pieces of my dream with Ellie Mae. She didn't understand it, but that was okay; she was a good listener. After I finished eating, she went to do some laundry, and I sat in the kitchen, recalling every detail of my nocturnal encounter. I thought long and hard about what my dad had said: "Uncle Joe will teach you, but you have to ask him." Almost without thinking, I found myself walking down the hallway toward Uncle Joe's office.

I knocked, but there was no answer. Pushing open the heavy door, I looked around, but the room was empty. I went straight to the table with the glass case. There it was—the book. Leaning in close, I could see that the binding was worn from being opened countless times.

So this is where my answers lie. Seventy-five years of cherished family history—three generations of wisdom—were locked away in this glass case. I pictured my Pop Angus writing down the secrets he'd learned from Papa James, putting them down on these pages with a feathered quill, by the light of an oil lamp on a desk in his library. My future was in this book—the key to my dreams of becoming the greatest prospector in the world.

I noticed a heavy iron latch that secured the glass cover, and I reached out and touched it, wishing it was not locked. Then, as my fingers brushed the metal, the lock clicked open. *That's odd, did Uncle Joe not close it firmly enough?*

The open latch stirred within me a deep-seated longing to fling open the case, claim the book, and prospect for the secrets hidden away inside. I lifted the glass cover, my hands shaking and my heart pounding in my chest. I reached out with my hand, and then paused, suddenly hesitant to touch this sacred tome. I felt like I was stealing a protected treasure. What if I touched it and it turned to ashes? Who was I to dare to open its pages?

I took a deep breath, my resolve returning, and grasped the book. It felt firm in my hand, solid, *real*. As I lifted it out of the case, I marveled at how light it was. This book held my future; shouldn't it be more substantial? I placed it on the edge of the oval table, being careful not to disturb its pages or damage its cover, my breath coming hard and fast.

A voice shattered the moment, jerking me back from the edge of fortune. "Laura!"

Uncle Joe was standing there, framed by the doorway. I was reminded of my first visit to that office. Once again, I'd been caught red-handed. My heart, already racing with excitement, skipped a beat in fright as I turned around. "Uncle Joe, you startled me."

Without a word, he crossed the room, picked up the book, placed it on his desk, and sat beside it, his hand resting protectively on the cover. "Please, Laura, sit down. It seems we need to talk."

I walked over to the couch, uncertain what to expect, never taking my eyes off the book, and sat down. "I get it now."

"You get what, Laura?"

"It's the book. It's all about that book," I replied. His gaze didn't waver; he was waiting for some type of explanation. I took a deep breath. *Here goes.* "You have to teach me the six secrets, Uncle Joe. I'm ready. Tell me the secrets! I need to know." It came out of me in a rush. This, I knew, was what I had been searching for.

Uncle Joe's tone was infuriatingly calm. "Laura—" he began, but I cut him off before he could continue. I was so eager to find out what those secrets were. I had to convince him to tell me.

"Dad told me that it was important for me to stay in Chicago if I was to become the greatest prospector in the world, and that you would be my mentor."

He frowned, puzzled. "You never told me that." He shifted in his seat. "When did your dad tell you that, Laura?"

"Last night," I replied, ignoring his raised eyebrows. "Yes, last night! He came to me in a dream. We were at the river, drinking coffee."

Uncle Joe clearly had no idea what to make of my story.

"I want you to teach me," I said firmly. "I will submit to whatever you tell me. You name it, and I will do it. Please, Uncle Joe, I'm begging you!"

"Laura, the change in you is proof enough that *something* happened. I've never heard you speak so positively, or appear so excited about your future. What it was, whether dream or premonition, I do not know. What I *do* know, however, is that you're a Dunagan and prospecting is in your blood."

"I *am* a Dunagan," I said, head held high.

"Yes, you are," he said, smiling. "That means that you must learn the same way I did, from Pop Angus. No shortcuts and no hurrying the process."

"I understand," I replied, my heart singing. He was saying yes! I could barely contain my excitement.

"You must understand: how much I tell you, when I tell you, and how I tell you is solely up to me. You do not decide when you're ready—I do. But don't mistake me. Your progress will influence my decisions. You must apply yourself. Follow the instructions precisely. Be patient, but not passive. Can you agree to those terms?"

"I can," I assured him. *I'm doing it, Dad!*

"You will face obstacles, distractions, detours, and disappointments. You will be tempted to give up, or to stop trying. You must realize that each obstacle is a stepping stone to your goals; each distraction is a springboard to your future; each detour is a sign that you are headed in the right direction; and each disappointment is proof that your dream is still before you."

He stood, never releasing my gaze. "You must shake off every hindrance and stay focused on the prize. This is the only path to the six secrets."

He picked up the book. His voice was reverent as he said, "You don't choose the book; the book chooses you. It is an honor and a privilege to be chosen. Take it to heart, and you will become the greatest prospector. This is your destiny!"

I felt like I had joined a secret order of knights. I was humbled to be chosen.

"Do you accept the prospecting challenge?" he asked as he placed the book back on his desk.

I nodded. "I do."

"All right then," he said, clapping his hands together. "You start tomorrow."

"With secret number one?" I asked, hoping against hope that it would be that simple.

Uncle Joe laughed. "No, you start work tomorrow. I have contacts in the Singer Company; you are going to be a salesgirl."

"Singer? Selling sewing machines?" I asked in disbelief.

"That's right," he said, a little smile tugging at the corner of his mouth.

"No way!" I shook my head. "That's not me, Uncle Joe. I'm no salesperson." I looked at him. "Can you really see me convincing people to do *anything?* Let alone spend money? Besides, I do better when I stay away from people. Just ask the man from the *Tribune.*"

"What man?" he asked, his grin spreading.

I looked away. "Never mind. I'm trying to save you the embarrassment. I will fail, miserably, and I am tired of failure."

"You'll do fine," he said, a small smile evident beneath his mustache.

"Do fine? Are you kidding me? I don't know a thing about sewing or sewing machines. Ask anyone! Ask Aunt Debra! I'm no lady."

Uncle Joe didn't react to my outburst. Instead, he reached into the middle drawer of his desk, retrieved a pen, and then jotted down a name and address for me to use the next day.

He handed me the paper with an air of finality and said, "It's done. They'll be expecting you tomorrow at 8 a.m."

I was hesitant to take the paper. "I don't have a choice, do I?"

"I can't *make* you do anything," Uncle Joe conceded. "However, you made a commitment: you agreed to my terms. There is no other path, if you wish to learn the six secrets of prospecting."

"What does selling sewing machines have to do with prospecting?" I shot back.

"Everything," he replied, his half-smile returning.

I swallowed, deflated. This was not what I had pictured.

Uncle Joe must have seen my inner struggle, because he came over and sat beside me. "Laura, do you remember what we talked about during your first visit to this office? I told you about the time Pop asked your dad and me to go to Chicago. I thought he had lost his mind. Prospecting gold was my ambition in life; to do anything else seemed ludicrous. But Pop wasn't crazy. He knew that if we would follow the six secrets, we would discover the true meaning of success."

Uncle Joe pointed to the awards and pictures on the walls around us and asked, "Do you think I accomplished all this because I was qualified, skilled, or experienced enough when I started?"

He didn't leave time for me to answer his question. "The truth is: I did not have a clue how to sell anything or build a business. But I followed these six secrets," he said, placing a hand on the book. "Everything I own—this house, the automobiles, the money, and the success—all comes from the book. And more than that: this book taught me how to cultivate lasting relationships, which span the globe. It has enabled me to travel and explore life, and it has provided resources for hospitals and orphanages; built homes and apartments for underprivileged families; clothed and fed the needy; constructed churches, soup kitchens, food pantries, and YMCAs all over Chicago; and so much more.

"These six secrets are not just about how to *get* more; they teach how to *give* more. If we don't seek ways to help people, we have lost the purpose of prospecting. This book contains the secrets to bringing happiness and hope. That's what Papa James and Pop Angus learned and passed down to me. Now you too have the opportunity to change the world."

Uncle Joe's words captivated my heart. I imagined myself handing out toys to poor children at Christmas, and I was ashamed that I had rejected this first challenge so quickly. My resolution returned.

"I'll be there at 7:45 a.m.," I promised.

"That's my girl," he encouraged. "I knew you were a Dunagan!"

"Yes, sir." I grinned.

"Now you're ready."

I nodded. "I'll learn how to sell sewing machines." I swallowed hard. *I can do this. Dad wanted me to do this.*

"I meant, you're ready for the first secret. Here it is: *Dress For The Weather.*"

He was giving me information from the book! I repeated the words, internally, memorizing them. *Dress For The Weather.* I wasn't sure what that had to do with selling sewing machines, but I figured Uncle Joe was going to explain.

After a moment, he smiled. "Laura, do you remember what you wore when we left Alaska?"

"I'll never forget. My feet were sore for a week." I chuckled, and Uncle Joe grinned.

"You sure did make a statement."

I lowered my head, embarrassed, but also proud of how I had stuck to my decision. "I was stubborn, all right."

"Just a little," he smiled. "But if you'll recall, I never said a word about it."

I nodded. "I remember."

"I thought it was outstanding that you were determined to be true to yourself, no matter what anyone said. Yet, at the same time, it was a pretty foolish choice of outfits."

I opened my mouth to explain, but he didn't give me a chance. "I knew what you were doing, and I knew the statement you hoped to make." His eyes took on a faraway look and he said, "I have panned for gold in the worst conditions you can imagine. Papa's experience panning in California was quite different from panning in Alaska. There, the conditions, weather, and season determined what was worn to work each day.

"For instance, Papa James did not wear the same outfit that my dad did. The weather in San Francisco was not at all like the weather in Sitka or Dawson City. I still remember my blue denim work pants. We did not have bib overalls like you wore. We held our pants up by suspenders or belts and there were no belt loops. Some trousers had a buckle or lace holes in the back for extra tightening.

"Prospectors in Sitka wore shirts made from a variety of animal hides, such as deer or elk, or from fabrics such as wool, cotton, linen, or linsey-woolsey, a mixture of wool and linen. The curved armhole, common in long-sleeved shirts today, was a novelty back then. The dominant style involved a 'drop shoulder.' Collars were a separate piece from the rest of the shirt. Prospectors would normally wear red or blue shirts to work, saving white shirts for dressy occasions.

"Long John pants were the underwear of choice, worn beneath wool trousers. At other times, the popular undergarment was short pants, fastened with a button fly and sometimes a belt in the back.

"Your dad and I wore sack coats, cut at mid-thigh, or tail coats in a variety of patterns. Pop Angus liked the blue and black tailcoats that were a common sight in the evenings. 'Duster' overcoats, made of oilcloth, were a popular way to keep the rain off, and we had those too.

"The hats the prospectors wore had low crowns and wide brims and were made of straw or felt. Before we moved to Alaska, I seldom saw Pop wear a hat. But there, every prospector I met wore a hat. And a scarf—do not forget the scarf! It came in handy on a windy day. I wore high wader boots with medium-height heels and squaring at the toes, similar to what you wore. Did you ever go into the river without your waders?"

I wasn't sure what this had to do with anything, but I told him about the one time I slipped and fell into the river without my waders on. "The water was freezing! Dad always taught me to dress warm and stay dry."

"So, what does this have to do with the first secret of success?" Uncle Joe voiced my unspoken question. "In the same way, to achieve effective sales and win business with a prospect, you have to prepare for the conditions. My father taught me that, when it comes to selling, you must dress for success, because you never get a second chance to make a first impression. Always *be your best* and anticipate how others will perceive you. That includes how you dress; your care for personal hygiene; the way you act, both in public and among friends; how you communicate with those around you; and how you present yourself. You are the product, and if prospects are not interested in you, they will also be uninterested in what you are offering."

"Dress for the weather. Be your best. First impressions are imperative," I repeated, trying to distill what he had said to its bare essentials.

"If you can apply this secret, you will increase your odds in sales and create your own opportunities. So choose your attire for tomorrow with care. As you go about your first day, think about the first impression you want to make with each person you meet. Give people eye contact. Do not dominate conversations, but don't be afraid to participate.

"When introduced to someone, use that person's name at least three times in the initial exchange; that will help you remember it. Ask questions. Let others tell you about *them*; only then will they care about you. Tomorrow will be your first lesson."

"I'm ready," I said, although I didn't feel it.

7

Door to Door

WHEN I ARRIVED AT THE address Uncle Joe had given me, I had a hard time finding a parking place. It had snowed the night before, and mountains of dirty snow lined the streets where cars might have parked. When I finally found a place, wedged between two snowdrifts, I had only five minutes to locate the Singer building. Firmly suppressing my rising panic and frustration, I straightened my mink fur hat and smoothed my wool coat with its matching collar and cuffs.

I had spent several hours the previous night choosing the right clothes—*dress for the weather,* Uncle Joe had said. *Be your best.* I was happy with what I'd chosen. Under the warm, elegant coat, my white, long-sleeved, silk turtleneck was partially covered by a half-sleeved cotton blouse. A long skirt hid all but the bottoms of my dark rayon stockings, worn inside my Mary Jane shoes. The shoes even had a bow. Okay, maybe they weren't the best choice for snow, but I understood that the secret wasn't just to be taken literally. And they looked good. Taking a deep breath, I marched toward the door.

The receptionist gave me a nametag to enter the facility, which reminded me of the *Chicago Tribune*. They had given me a nametag there, too, until I was demoted, and then they'd taken it back. I pushed my swelling irritation aside. This would be different.

I took the elevator to the fourth floor, as instructed, where I was greeted by a tall, thin man in a gray suit and a crew cut.

"You must be Laura," he said.

"I am."

"I'm Mr. Dawson, but you can call me Ken." He smiled.

"It's a pleasure to meet you, Mr. Dawson."

"Ken, please." We exchanged smiles, but mine felt forced. *This guy better not be flirting with me.*

Ken took me to a long, narrow conference room. I felt ridiculous, sitting alone at the big table in one of a dozen chairs, a daunting array of forms spread out before me. I assaulted the task, filling out every form to the best of my ability, signing my name more than twenty times. Was this really necessary? I was going to be a salesgirl, not a guard to the president.

I must have been faster than I thought, because I sat alone in the room for an additional half hour before Ken returned. He picked up the stack of forms and said, "Okay, we're ready to get started."

I followed him out to an open room where there were about ten sewing machines secured to a large workbench, with stools in front of each station. At first, I was confused. *I'm selling these things, not making clothes, right?*

Ken stopped abruptly, spun to face me, and clapped his hands. "So, Laura, how much do you know about sewing machines?"

I felt a smile pull at my mouth, but I kept it from showing as I replied, "Well, I've seen them in a catalog, I think."

He looked taken aback, so I quickly reassured him. "I'm joking."

Clearly relieved, he said, "Oh, you scared me for a second."

The unfortunate thing was, I hadn't been joking at all. I had never seen a sewing machine, let alone operated one.

Ken regained his composure and continued. "So you are familiar with sewing machines, right? After all, aren't you a woman?"

It took a great effort not to say what I was thinking. But I held my tongue and said, "I sure am!" with a small, playful laugh. *Be your best, be your best*, I chanted in my mind.

Ken continued, unaware of my internal struggle. "You know how they work, right?" He wasn't going to continue without an answer. I needed to think fast.

"Well, as I understand it, they're not all the same." I was panning blind, but I prayed for a miracle.

"That's true!" he replied. "And our models certainly aren't the same as any old sewing machine. Why don't I give you a demonstration and a basic tutorial?"

Gold! I struck gold. "That would be wonderful."

He smiled, clearly enjoying the idea of helping me. He pointed out several machines, giving their names, model numbers, and a brief history of their origins. I would be selling the Red Eye, model 66, so Ken walked me through each step, from weaving the thread through the machine and down to the needle, to filling bobbins with thread from a spool. Though he only explained the more complicated concepts, I was able to watch closely and learn the simpler tasks as well: how to replace needles, attach the bobbin, and start the sewing machine's electric engine. Once he had completed his tutorial, he took several pieces of fabric from a nearby pile and demonstrated the machine's ability to sew through any thickness.

"Do you mind if I give a try?" I asked.

"Of course not," Ken smiled. "Have at it!"

I pressed the pedal too hard and the machine raced out of control, causing the needle to plunge through the fabric at an alarming rate.

"Hold on there, it's not a race!"

I looked away, letting my shame show. "I've never actually used an electric machine before."

"Oh!" Ken said, instantly sympathetic. "Why didn't you say so?"

For the next two hours, I practiced sewing. At first, Ken helped me get a feel for the machine, and then he left me to practice, saying simply, "You need to be able to use all versions of this model; times are changing, and electric machines are growing in popularity."

By the end of the session, I felt like a pro and also felt ready to go sell my first sewing machine.

Ken returned just before lunch hour and gave me a demo version of the Singer 66 machine, some paperwork, and a printed advertisement to leave with potential customers. He also gave me a list of addresses for potential customers in the area. I carried the thirty-pound beast out to my car and drove to the neighborhood Ken had assigned to me.

I felt confident and grown up. I was dressed for success and ready to make a good impression and sell a sewing machine.

After I had parked, I read through the materials Ken had given me. Then I marched up the driveway of the first house on my list. I knocked and a woman in her middle sixties came to the door. Smiling as brightly as I could, I announced, "Hello, my name is Laura Dunagan, and I am here to sell you this beautiful Singer 66 sewing machine!"

"Who are you?" the woman asked, obviously hard of hearing.

"Laura. Laura Dunagan," I repeated, a little louder.

"And what's that in your hand?" she asked.

"It's your sewing machine," I replied, standing straight, a smile hiding my hesitation.

"I didn't order any sewing machine." She shut the door in my face.

I wanted to pound on the door and give her a piece of my mind, but I took a deep breath instead, then retraced my steps down the driveway and approached the next house.

"Hi, I'm Laura, and I have a Singer 66 sewing machine I would like to show you."

"I already have one," this woman claimed.

"I bet you don't have one like this," I replied, smiling.

"No, I have a Sears and Roebuck," she declared.

"But this one has a new improved motor—"

SLAM! She shut the door in my face. *Well, if that's how it is . . .* Again, I retraced my steps.

As I approached the third house, I was determined to get a sale. A woman answered the door in her nightgown and slippers, with curlers in her hair, although it was two o'clock in the afternoon.

"Good afternoon, ma'am," I began.

"Oh, honey, don't call me ma'am; that sounds so old."

"I apologize. My name is Laura Dunagan, and I would like ten minutes of your time to explain the value and benefit of a Singer 66 sewing machine."

"Well—"

"I'm sure you want to save money, and I have just the thing that will do it."

"I'm not—"

"You're ready! I can see it in your eyes, and you won't regret it, either."

"But—"

I lifted my hand. "No buts. I insist that you make your husband happy and save your household money."

"If you could—"

"I can and will help you get a great deal on this machine!"

"I don't know—"

"Sure you do! You are a woman of culture. You want one! And you can make payments, if you like. Why not let me in, and we can sign you up for one today. It will be delivered by next week! What do you say?"

"Can I talk now?" The woman had one hand on her hip and was tapping her foot.

"Sure you can," I said, beaming.

"What I was trying to say, before you interrupted me, was that I'm not the owner; I'm just a houseguest. If you could come back tomorrow, you might catch Mrs. Davis. She might be interested." She looked me up and down. "But I don't think so. You're pushy. Scat!"

SLAM! She shut the door.

Before I had a chance to turn or walk away, the door flew open again. "And I'm not married!" SLAM!

I went to a few more houses on that street, with no success, before deciding to try my luck around the next block. I approached a bungalow home with two large pillars flanking the front porch and flowers pots hanging everywhere. *Surely, this homeowner works around the house, so she must be interested in a sewing machine.*

There was a woman kneeling on the porch, so I walked up to her. She had her back to me as she crouched down, tending to a plant. I realized that she had not heard me approaching, so I cleared my throat. When she didn't react, I said, "Good afternoon!"

She jumped upright, slipping backward off the top step, smashing her pot in the process.

I caught her, mid-fall. "I'm so sorry; I didn't intend to startle you." I helped her to her feet. "Are you all right?" I continued to hold her steady.

"I think so." She seemed uncertain.

"Here, sit down," I suggested.

She sat down on one of the two patio chairs on the porch, and I claimed the other chair and launched into my sales pitch. This time, I figured, I would take the fast approach and remove the cover from the sewing machine, forcing the potential buyer to see its beauty and benefits. I placed the case on a small table and lifted the cover with a flourish. "Isn't she a beauty?"

She leaned forward to take a closer look.

"Look here," I said, as I pointed to the neck of the machine. "This is the thread take-up lever. And these are the tension discs, and if we follow the thread through this eyehole into the needle, past the needle presser foot, through the point of hook—it ends here in the bobbin case. This here, this is the bobbin ejector."

I stepped back, pretty impressed with myself for remembering everything. "So, what do you think?"

She paused, looked at the sewing machine, then looked up at me. "Who are you, again?"

"I'm Laura," I answered, slumping slightly. Would I ever get a sale?

"You're dressed pretty fancy for a repairperson, with that fur and all."

"Oh no, ma'am. I'm not the repairperson. I'm a salesperson. I sell sewing machines."

She leaned back. "Well, my sewing machine is broken. I thought you came to fix it."

"Sounds like you could use a new one," I pressed.

"I don't need a new one. I need someone to fix the one I've got!" Her voice took on a tone of frustration. "Can you fix it?"

"No, ma'am, I can't."

"Well, call your boss and get them to send me someone who can!"

"I'll see what I can do." I lowered the cover back into place and fastened the latches on each side. I had picked up my case and started walking down the steps, when she said, "Don't forget me now."

"I'll do my best to forget *you*, lady," I murmured under my breath as I walked down the steps and sidewalk. I was discouraged and frustrated. *This is stupid,* I thought. *Why am I doing this?*

I continued going door to door. At some places there was no one home and others would not let me inside for a demonstration. I tried different approaches, but each time I got the same result—no sale. It was almost four-thirty in the afternoon, and I was nearing the end of my rope. However, I resolved to try one more house before I stopped for the day.

I approached the door with all the confidence I could muster. *You can do this, Laura. You've got this! Be your best!* I thought about Uncle Joe's words: *You don't get a second chance with a first impression.*

I focused my thoughts and knocked. A woman about my age answered the door.

"Hi, I'm Laura, and I'm a sales representative for Singer. I came out today to offer you a great opportunity, which is to be the first in your neighborhood to purchase a Red Eye 66."

"If I'm the *first* in the neighborhood, does that mean no one else wanted one?" she asked.

"Well, I haven't covered the entire neighborhood, but yes, you would be the first to buy from me. If you could give me ten minutes of your time for a demonstration, I'm sure you will like the new and improved features in this latest model."

The next question stopped me in my tracks. I had been a fool not to expect it. "Do you sew?"

Don't fail now! "I was sewing for a couple of hours earlier today, as a matter of fact."

"Is that right?" she replied, smiling.

Oh, no. She suspects! "Yes, it is." I nodded emphatically.

"Okay. How long have you been sewing?" she pried, leaning against the doorframe.

"Not as long as I would like," I deflected. I needed to take control of this conversation, fast! "If my mom was still living, we'd do it together. But it's just not the same without her."

"I'm sorry for your loss—my condolences." She stood straight once more, and seemed sincere.

I bowed my head. "Thank you." *That was close!*

"I'm just curious," she said, her tone less sharp but still questioning. "Do you own one?"

"I haven't bought this latest model—electric machines are still new to me—but they are so much more convenient!" *That's it. Aim for the sale.*

"No, I mean do you own a sewing machine?"

Drat. Well, the truth had failed me. "I sure do." However, the instant I spoke the lie, I felt ashamed. What would Dad think if he knew I made my first sale with a lie?

I sighed, looking down. "No, that was a lie. To be honest, I don't own one." I reached down, grabbed the sewing carrier by the handle, lifted it, and looked up to meet her gaze. "Thank you for your time. You have a great day."

I turned and walked off, leaving her standing in her doorway.

As I walked down the street to my car, I wanted to cuss out loud. I had walked ten blocks and knocked on forty-three doors, all without making one single sale. But I knew I could do better, so I refrained. I placed the sewing machine in the back seat and drove off.

The icing on the cake was the traffic. Downtown Chicago was at a standstill as more snow fell and everyone tried to get out early. *Great, now I'll never get home.*

Sitting in the car, I relived my first day as a salesgirl. Forty-three rejections. I'd been mistaken for a repairperson, called pushy, chased by a dog, ignored, and laughed at.

As the traffic inched forward, I realized I was only a few blocks from Uncle Joe's downtown office. He was never home before six o'clock. *He's still at work. Seeing him can't be worse than this traffic.*

Uncle Joe owned and operated one of the largest and most successful insurance companies in Chicago. Working with banks and brokers, he was able to offer insurance to manufacturers, unions, construction and transport companies, and to farmers in Illinois and the Midwest.

The receptionist's desk was empty as I walked through the lobby. In fact, I was able to get all the way to Uncle Joe's office without seeing another person.

When I pushed the door open, Uncle Joe looked up from his desk, a smile spreading across his face. "Well, look who it is!" He came over and gave me a hug. He then stepped back, looked at my outfit, and said, "Doesn't she look beautiful!"

I grinned, feeling a little better.

"How was your first day?" he asked.

My grin faded. "I followed your advice, but it got me nowhere! I wore all the right clothes. I was polite and pleasant. I spent two hours studying a sewing machine, learning every part and piece of my product."

I took a deep breath, feeling heat rising in my cheeks. "I dressed for success. I was confident. I made good first impressions. And not one person wanted to buy a sewing machine. I don't get it! I did everything you said."

He started laughing.

I glared at him. "It's not funny, Uncle Joe. It was horrible!"

Still chuckling, he waved his hand, signaling me to follow him. "Come with me."

I followed him to the kitchen and break room. He poured us cups of coffee. It looked to have been in the pot all day. I wanted to punch a wall or kick a dog. I needed to get the frustration out of my system.

"So, you know your product?" he asked, sitting down at one of the tables.

"Oh, yes. I do." I sat down across from him, realizing I had actually carried the demo sewing machine up there with me, without thinking.

I lifted the beast, set it on the table between us, took the case off, and started explaining the mechanism to him in great detail.

"Did you tell them all this?" he asked, that smile tugging at the corner of his mouth again.

"Not everyone, but *almost* everyone."

Uncle Joe started chuckling, but he regained his composure when I glared at him. He took a sip of his coffee, looked into my eyes, and said something that would stay with me the rest of my life: "People don't care how much you *know* until they know how much you *care*! And people won't buy from you until they know you and like you.

"The next time you go on a sales call, get to know the person first. Ask her questions. Ask about the things you see around her home—that is how you will get to know her better. Win her over *before* you try to get something from her, especially if you are trying to make a sale."

I blushed again, remembering the woman I'd barely allowed to speak—the one who didn't even live there and who didn't have a husband. A few questions would have helped me out there, for sure.

"Did you see the offices here when you came in?"

I nodded.

"Do you know why we are located here?"

I shook my head, taking a swig of coffee.

"I don't pay rent to be here. The owners of this building actually pay me, because my company's reputation draws other tenants.

"And do you know why we have such a good reputation? Before *anyone* gives me a penny for insurance, I take time to get to know them, or one of my people does. We become acquainted, build rapport, and develop and cultivate healthy relationships. Relationships build businesses, not money. If you do not have relationships, people won't give you their money!

"I first learned this from Pop Angus when I worked in the country store back in Seattle. Going thorough inventories, keeping prices competitive, and managing the books were not what made our business grow. Pop believed that knowing your customers was more important than knowing your product. In fact, if you think about it correctly, people *are* your product. That's prospecting.

"Prospecting is nothing more than getting to know people. We do it every day; we just don't see it. You are prospecting when you strike up a conversation with a person—anywhere and anytime. Laura, to improve as a salesgirl, you need to develop relationships. People won't buy from you unless they know you, like you, and trust you. Being your best is not just about your appearance—it's about how well you listen to and connect with your prospects. Getting somebody to like and trust you is the secret to closing any deal."

Uncle Joe took another sip of coffee and seemed to decide something. "Are you ready for secret number two?" he asked.

I sat up straight, my tough day forgotten. It was time to learn more.

8

Know What You're Looking For

"WHEN PROSPECTING FOR GOLD, HOW did your Dad know where to pan?"

Now this was territory I knew. "First, he surveyed the area to see if the right markers were there. He took samples of the soil or rock beds, testing them to learn about what he might find." I could picture my dad on the riverbank, calling out  to me when he found positive signs, his excitement bubbling over.

Uncle Joe leaned back, smiling. "You mean he didn't just jump into the river and start panning for gold?"

I shook my head. "Of course not! I remember one time when Dad and I were prospecting and he stopped by a big tree with its roots hanging over the bank, down into the water. He took a shovelful of dirt and dumped it on the bank. Then he used his pan to sift through the dirt, and sure enough, there was some gold. He was a master at it, Uncle Joe."

"Yes, he was," he said, smiling.

"And we never prospected where we first found gold. We always followed the river and searched for the source."

"That's right, Laura," Uncle Joe interjected. "Which brings us to secret number two: *Know What You're Looking For.*"

I had retrieved a notebook and pen from my purse and copied down this second nugget from the book of secrets, as I called it.

"Think of it this way," Uncle Joe added. "The rivers of Alaska are spread out and the source could be miles away. But it all flows downstream. So when we found little chunks of gold in silt where we were panning, Pop always said to walk straight up the river. If there was more to be found, and if luck was on our side, we would find that source. That is where the biggest discoveries would be waiting. We needed to carefully choose where we would pan and take note of what conditions make for a favorable location."

"I understood that," I said, crossing my arms over my chest. "But what does that have to do with selling sewing machines?"

"Everything," Uncle Joe replied. "When it comes to selling something, so many people just jump into the river at the first place they find, never taking the time to put together a plan. What made your dad different from thousands of other prospectors was that he learned that not every stream had gold, and that if he could find the right location, he would not lose precious time and profits.

"When prospecting for sewing machine sales, what you need to do first is make a prospect list, a summary of the type of person you believe needs your product as well as a list of specific people: people you know from college, the women you ate lunch with at the *Tribune*, and co-workers from the Mercantile. Your list becomes your target market. A target market is a group of customers who are more likely to purchase your product or service. If you stay focused on your *target market*, people who need a sewing machine, your chances of having them purchase one will increase enormously. When it comes to sales, many people fail—not from lack of effort, but because they waste so much time and do not generate enough leads to make a profit.

"They run around trying to prospect everyone they meet, putting themselves in awkward, humiliating, and embarrassing situations, and taking an enormous amount of rejection while getting little or no results. They are wasting their time and energy by prospecting in the wrong river. That's why so many prospectors quit and left empty-handed. They ran out of energy or money. To be successful in your prospecting efforts, you need to look where the gold *is*, not where you wish it was."

"Like going through the suburbs door to door," I sighed, taking another swallow of the bitter coffee.

"There's nothing wrong with that," Uncle Joe responded. "But it will limit your success. You can go door to door, but if you can first find a community that is a target market, it will make a world of difference."

"If a real estate agent wants to sell a house right away, he is going to be thinking, 'Who are the likely first-time homebuyers?' So whom does he target? Kids coming out of college. He starts sending advertisements around to kids in their graduation packages. He goes to the biggest employers in town and creates relationships with those employers so that when they hire new people full time, they will pass him the lead. In any business, the same rules apply. Once you know your product, and once you know what you're looking for and what you have in your hand, then you can start thinking, 'Where are the prospects?'

"Pop used to say, 'Gold starts with a source.' When you find that source, you follow it upstream. In prospecting, the *source* is your list. Going *upstream* in sales is getting referrals. When you talk to your prospects or sell a sewing machine, always ask that person, 'Who do you know who might be interested in a sewing machine?' Constantly be building your list by asking for referrals. Referrals are a great way to build your list and have an endless supply of prospects. It's like prospecting for gold; you never know where the gold is unless you go upstream."

"So how do I find the target market for these sewing machines?" I asked, uncertain how to apply this secret effectively.

"In your case, I suggest you find places where women gather, get to know them and earn their trust, and then invite them to see a demonstration. Use your resources well and do only two or three demonstrations a week, with twenty-five women at one time. Then you encourage those same people to come back and bring a friend, and you do another demonstration for the guests they bring. That's prospecting your target market."

Uncle Joe finished his coffee while I sat, considering what he had said. After a moment, he set the cup aside and continued.

"Remember, when dealing with your prospects, always keep it relational. Listening is the key. As individuals tell you about themselves, their needs will surface. Good salespeople connect a need with an opportunity. That is when you can point out how the sewing machine will solve someone's problem.

"People always know when someone is giving them a sales pitch. Keep the focus on them and their needs, not on the sewing machine itself. Once you've captured a prospect's interest, invite her to a meeting."

I could already see myself sitting in front of a crowd of well-dressed ladies, who would stare with rapt attention as my needle flew across the fabric. Where would I find these women? I started thinking of places where women gather. The first thing that came to mind was Aunt Debra and her tea parties, community functions, and organizations she volunteered for and gave donations to. I pictured women in fabric stores and hair salons. I could do this!

I looked up and saw my own excitement mirrored in Uncle Joe's eyes. It was contagious. I felt the frustrations of the day falling away. Even the long, slow drive ahead didn't bother me anymore—I had plenty to keep my mind busy.

* * * * *

The next day, I walked into the office, confident that I was going to make at least one sale. "Good morning, Ken," I said, a gleam of excitement in my eye.

"Good morning, Laura," he said, smiling broadly.

"I want to buy a sewing machine. How do I get one?"

He frowned. "What's wrong with your demo?"

I waved his question aside. "Nothing is wrong with it. I simply want my own."

"Why?"

"Are you going to sell me one or not?"

"Okay, okay. No need to get huffy with me."

I sighed. "I'm sorry, Ken, but if I am going to sell sewing machines to others, I can't very well not have one myself." I paused. "One of this model, I mean."

"I never thought of that," he considered. "That's a great idea, Laura."

I purchased my demo and paid Ken for it before carrying it out to my car. With a firm determination building within me, I drove back to the same neighborhood I had walked through the day before.

As I parked, I noticed the elderly woman I had startled the day before was watering her plants again. I was happy to see her, because on my way over, I'd stopped at the hardware store to purchase a replacement pot. I felt guilty for causing her to break one.

I approached with the new pot in my hand. "Hello, there. Remember me?"

The woman turned to me, confused. "Should I?"

"I was here yesterday. I'm the one who scared you; you broke a pot."

She glanced at the hole in her arrangements, where the pot had been. "Oh, yes. I remember now."

With both hands, I extended the pot toward her. "This is to replace the broken one," I said. "I'm sorry."

She smiled, taking the pot and placing it on the porch. "You didn't have to do that. That was sweet of you. Would you like some lemonade?"

I sighed in relief. "I would love some."

She led me to her kitchen, pointing out the greenhouse in her backyard as we passed the window. "I was just getting my plants ready to move in there for the winter," she explained.

By asking a few questions, I found out that she was a widow, living alone. She had been married for forty-six years, had four children (all still living), and, through them, eighteen grandchildren and three great-grandchildren. She talked about her husband as if he were still alive, even though he had died six years earlier.

After about an hour, she suddenly asked, "Where's that sewing machine you showed me yesterday?"

I had left the demo in my car, bringing only the pot. "It's in my car, Mrs. Patterson."

"You know, dear, after you left, I went back to my sewing room—well, actually, it's a spare bedroom, but I like to call it my sewing room," she smiled. "I realized that that sewing machine broke a few months before my Walter died, and I haven't used it since." She paused for a moment. "My, how time flies."

"It sure does."

"Well, I want to show my granddaughters how to sew, but that old machine will probably never work again. Can you show me yours? I'm going to need a new one."

She loved the machine, and she wrote me a check on the spot so I could place her order as soon as possible. When she finished signing, I asked her, "Do you know anyone else who might be interested in a new sewing machine?"

She recommended two of her daughters—she wanted her granddaughters to be able to practice—and her neighbor, two houses down.

Walking back to my car, I felt like I was floating. I had sold my first sewing machine and obtained three solid leads! It was amazing what a glass of lemonade could produce. I hadn't even tried to make a sale. I just listened to her stories, laughed with her, and even cried once. As it turned out, Mrs. Patterson would become one of my greatest sources.

A week later, she took me to a church meeting. Then I went with her to her church's monthly women's luncheon to give demonstrations, and I sold twelve machines on the spot. We became friends, and I stopped by her house at least once a month for tea or a glass of lemonade. I had found my first source and followed it upstream. I was beginning to master secret number two: *Know What You Are Looking For!*

* * * * *

In my first month, I sold thirteen Singer sewing machines, a company record for a new salesperson. I won the Outstanding Salesperson award for that month and was recognized at the regional meeting in downtown Chicago. I was so thrilled—my first trophy! I had a long way to go before I could catch up to Uncle Joe's collection, but it was a start.

As I sat there in the ballroom at the hotel, waiting for my name to be called so I could go up and accept my award, I thought, *This selling thing is a piece of cake. I'll be back here next month.*

After my first month's success, however, my prospect list grew smaller, and soon I was having a hard time even getting in the door, much less doing demonstrations or making sales. I became frustrated because I thought Singer should supply me with an endless list of names of potential customers in my area. After several attempts to speak with a company representative, I was just told to talk to my friends and family members, something I had already done.

Then I thought about the second secret: *Know What You Are Looking For.* I thought I knew who my prospective customers were, but the problem was, I didn't know where to find them. I decided to visit a couple of new neighborhoods. I should have checked with Ken to see if the areas I selected were good ones, but I was too stubborn to ask for help. I'd approach them like

Dad approached the rivers, I thought, and look for signs. I *knew* I would sell twenty-five sewing machines in my second month.

I went to my first home and knocked on the door. A woman with a quizzical look on her face opened it. "Hi, how are you today?" I asked. She just stared at me, while six young children peered at me around her skirts.

"Oh my, we have a houseful, don't we?" I said, trying to be warm and friendly.

The children started giggling and ran back inside. "Bye," I called after them.

The mother looked down at my demo case.

I took that as a question. "Oh, this? This is a sewing machine."

She continued to stare.

"I imagine buying clothes for six children is a challenge these days, isn't it? Many women tell me they're making their own clothes and saving a lot of money."

She said nothing.

I felt my cheeks burning, but pressed on. "Can I have a few moments of your time to demonstrate how it works?"

She crossed her arms, looking irritated.

I'm getting too pushy. I need to slow down and let her know I care. "I love your hat—bonnet—whatever you call it. Did you make it yourself?"

She smiled, but still said nothing. Now I was getting frustrated. *I wish she would just slam the door in my face instead of staring.* I took a deep breath. *One more try:* "Nice weather we're having, wouldn't ya say?" *Say something, lady; you're killing me here.*

"*Ich kann Dich nicht verstehen,*" she muttered.

"Excuse me?"

"*Ich kann nicht Englisch sprechen,*"

I started laughing aloud and could not stop. Clearly this woman didn't understand a word of English. She was probably as frustrated as I was!

"You have a nice day," I told her as I left, although I'm sure she had no idea what it meant. At each house in that neighborhood, I heard the same things: "*Ich kann nicht Englisch sprechen,*" and, "*Nein, danke.*" By the end of the day, all I had to show for my efforts were sore feet and aching arms.

The next morning, I went to the office and decided to get a good laugh out of my previous day's adventures.

"Ken, I went to Jefferson Park on the northwest side, but I could not understand anyone there."

He chuckled. "Do you know why?"

"Why?" I asked.

"Because that's Germantown."

"Seriously?"

"Yep," he declared, his grin spreading wider. "One out of every four Chicagoans was either born in Germany or had a parent born there."

I put a hand on my hip. "What are you, a walking encyclopedia?"

"No, I read it in the *Chicago Tribune*. Ever heard of it?" He smirked.

I rolled my eyes. "Very funny."

"Why don't you try going to the southwest side? There are no Germans living there."

* * * * *

On the southwest side, I learned the words for "no thanks" in Polish: "*Nie, dziękuję.*" At first, I wanted to kill Ken, but as I returned to the office, I calmed down and was even able to laugh it off.

When I arrived, Ken was grinning from ear to ear. "Any Germans?"

I glared, and he laughed.

Once he had composed himself, he pointed to a map on his desk, and then he helped me choose a new area to canvass—English-speaking, this time, and the kind of neighborhood where people had money and could afford to buy sewing machines. With a renewed sense of hope, I grabbed my demo case first thing the next morning and headed out.

By the end of the day, I was deflated again. I couldn't get even one person to commit. No one would even allow me to demonstrate the machine. These women all had sewing machines already. I was beginning to think the people in this area made too much money.

The week ended, and still I had not made a sale. That was my third no-sale week in a row, and I had only one more week left until the month would end. I thought about the previous month and winning the award. *What am I going to say when people ask me how many I sold this month?*

What am I doing wrong? I replayed in my mind everything Uncle Joe had said. *Know what you are looking for. Find places where women gather. When you make a sale, ask for referrals.* That was what I'd done the first month, and it had worked so well. But when my prospect list dried up, I'd gone back to the door-to-door approach, without even doing my research properly on the neighborhoods I was visiting. I needed to go upstream. But where to start? Out of sheer desperation, I returned to Mrs. Patterson's neighborhood, hoping it would bring me good fortune. *Maybe I can get another chance at the women's luncheon.*

* * * * *

"Hi, Mrs. Patterson," I said, as I walked up the front porch steps. "I'm just passing by to see how your sewing machine is working for you."

"Just great." She beamed. "I love it!"

Unfortunately, I soon found out that I'd come too late—the women's luncheon had been held the previous week. But on seeing my disappointment, Mrs. Patterson said, "You know, now that I think about it, some of the ladies from the neighborhood are meeting at Mrs. Collins's house this Saturday. We meet once a month. Everyone brings yarn, and we knit or crochet—whatever we wish. Maybe you could come and show us your machine then?"

"Saturday it is." I smiled. *Thank goodness.* I was following the river upstream again.

9

Use the Right Tools

AS I WALKED AWAY FROM Mrs. Patterson's, I noticed a woman a few houses down sweeping snow away from her gate as her husband shoveled the walk. I recognized her. *She's the one who asked me if I owned a sewing machine.* When I was close enough for her to hear the click of my heels on the sidewalk, she turned and stopped, broom in hand. "Aren't you the sewing lady?"

I stopped too, smiling. "Yes. And I'm happy to tell you, I'm now the proud owner of a Singer Red Eye 66. I bought one the next day. Might you be interested now in seeing a demonstration?" I asked.

"Actually, I bought one two weeks ago."

"Really?" *Huh, but she was too good for me?*

"Yes. I got your phone number from Mrs. Patterson. I called the sales office three times, but I never heard back from you. It worked out anyways. Ken called me, and then he came out to the house and gave me a demonstration. Such a nice young man."

"Ken?"

"Yes. I liked your passion, so I wanted to buy from you. But Ken said it didn't matter who sold it, just so long as I was happy."

That snake. I was burning inside and trying my best not to show it. Every salesperson made a commission on each sale. *Ken stole my customer. How many times has this happened? That's why I haven't made any sales this month—he stole my referrals!*

* * * * *

The next day, I stormed into the sales office. "Ken!" He turned, startled by my tone. When I saw him, I pointed and said, "Yeah, you!"

He lifted his hands. "I know. I'm the only Ken who works here, Laura."

"This is no time for jokes."

"Someone steal your coffee this morning? What's wrong with you?"

"You're what's wrong!"

"Me? What did I do?" He glanced about as people stared.

"You're a thief." I poked him in the chest. "You stole my customer. And don't try to deny it, because she told me she called the sales office for me, but you went to her house and sold her a machine, right out from under me!"

"I don't know where you got your information, but I followed company policy. If a customer does not receive a call back from the sales representative after three attempts, the sale must be fulfilled within twenty-four hours by the office manager. I'm the office manager."

I stepped back, a little shocked. "Why didn't I know about that?"

"Well, it is in our company policy book—the one you received and signed for the day you were hired. And just in case you haven't had time to read it, we repeat the top ten rules each Monday morning at our sales meeting. You know, the meeting you skip every week." He was calm now, realizing that my shouting was done.

"Even so, you could have at least told me." My defense was dissolving before my eyes.

"Laura, do you even check your messages?"

Messages. Oh, no! The message box! Each employee had a message box.

"You don't, do you?" He smiled, shaking his head. "Every time a customer calls and specifically asks for a sales representative, it is company policy to place the contact information in the sales representative's message box. Technically, company policy states that a salesperson who fails to respond after three requests is to receive a written warning, and if he or she accumulates more than three write-ups, it is grounds for termination."

I hung my head.

"But instead of writing you up, I fulfilled the orders. In fact, I didn't take the commission either."

I looked up at him in shock. "What?"

He looked down, almost seeming embarrassed. "The orders I filled for you this month will still go on your monthly bonus check. So you are going to get paid the commission, even though I did the work."

My cheeks grew hot. I had made an idiot of myself. No wonder my prospect list was dwindling. It was my fault, and I had lost opportunities and falsely accused a co-worker. It was good to know that Ken had my back and was trying to help me, but, if anything, that made me feel worse.

"Oh, Ken. I'm so sorry."

"Just check your messages from now on." His voice was quiet, resigned. "Laura, you are one of the smartest salespeople I have ever trained. You have the potential to become one of the greatest this company has ever had." He sighed. "I don't know what is going on with you right now, but I suggest you figure it out before you lose this opportunity."

Ignoring the knowing glances and chuckles from the other salespeople who'd been listening, I headed to the women's restroom. I washed my face, blew my nose, lifted my head, and looked at myself in the mirror. *The greatest prospector in the world. Yeah, right.*

I took the rest of the day off and called in sick the next day.

* * * * *

Saturday morning, I was due to give my demonstration at Mrs. Collins's home. I'd wanted to cancel, but Mrs. Patterson had gone out of her way to make this happen. I couldn't let her down.

It was a beautiful morning, crisp and clear, and the snow had melted enough for a group of kids to play baseball in the street. Their shouts and laughter followed me as I made my way up to Mrs. Collins's door and knocked. I set my demo case on the railing so I could introduce myself.

A silver-haired, rosy-cheeked woman with a warm smile opened the door and shook my outstretched hand. "It's so nice to meet you, Laura—do come in." I turned to retrieve my demo but heard a loud crack and saw a blur of white. Instinctively, I ducked, and the next thing I knew, my demo case hit the floor in front of me with a thud, breaking open so that the machine fell out.

The boys who had been playing baseball came running over, trying to find their missing ball. I wanted to choke one of them. However, I maintained my composure, gathered up my machine, and followed Mrs. Collins inside.

After a half hour or so of tea and small talk, the group of women eagerly gathered around me to watch the Singer in action. But when I plugged it in, the motor would not start. I checked and rechecked the machine, but I could not get it to work.

No one purchased a sewing machine that day, and I had not made a single sale on my own for the entire month. I was a failure. Everyone at work would be laughing at how far the Outstanding Salesperson had fallen. I walked to my car and climbed in, placing the broken case on the passenger seat, and sat there ready to cry. Then, suddenly, a man appeared at my window.

"Hi, are you Laura?" he asked.

I had never seen him before, at least not that I could remember. He opened my door and reached out his hand, saying, "Allow me." Tall and handsome, he had dark hair and wore a beige suit and smart wool coat, accompanied by a paisley tie and carefully buffed shoes. I'd always found men in suits faintly ridiculous, preferring boots and overalls, but for some reason this man's appearance had a different effect on me.

What does he want? I don't know why I did it, but I gave him my hand, and he helped me out of the car.

"Frank. Frank Roheny." He handed me his business card. I looked down at it and under his name it read: "Real Estate Agent/Attorney."

"You're going to love this house," he said as he walked me to the curb. "It's a two-bedroom, one bath, with a sunroom in the back. You probably already know, but sunrooms are hard to find in Chicago." I glanced in the direction he was looking and saw a "For Sale" sign stationed in the front yard. "Now, I know you wanted a three-bedroom," he continued. "But when you look inside, you will find a large pantry and laundry room in the rear of the house, which could easily be divided to create a small bedroom."

He stopped, turning to me. "How many children did you say you have?"

"Excuse me?"

"I apologize, Mrs. Martin. I can't recall how many children you said you have, when we spoke yesterday."

"I think you must have mistaken me for someone else."

He looked me up and down, clearly confused. "You're not Laura?"

"Yes, my name is Laura."

"Laura Martin?"

"No, Laura Dunagan."

"I thought—"

"I get it. You thought I was Laura Marshall."

"Martin."

"Martin." I shrugged.

He cleared his throat. "So you're not Laura Martin."

"That's correct."

"Then why did you get out of the car?"

"I had my reasons." Starting with the fact that since he'd appeared at my window, all the troubles of my past few weeks seemed to have evaporated. I stared into his dark brown eyes.

By now, another automobile had pulled up, and a woman who was presumably the real Mrs. Martin was walking toward us.

"How embarrassing." He stepped back, scratching his cheek.

"Not a problem—you're just doing your job."

"You have my card. If you are ever interested in a house, just give me a call."

"And if I'm not interested in a house, will you give me a call?" I winked.

His eyes grew big and his mouth opened. Obviously, he was not used to bold women. It wasn't a proper question, but I didn't care. Frank had caught my eye, and I wanted to see where it would take me.

I retrieved a pen from my pocketbook, wrote my name and phone number on the back of his card, and handed it back to him. "Call me." I turned and walked back to my car.

As I opened the door, I glanced back. He was staring down at his business card, an expression of disbelief on his face. I started my car, then looked back one more time, just as he lifted his head. Our eyes met and we both smiled. Needless to say, my ride home had a different tenor. I glanced down at the broken case, but it didn't bother me at all.

* * * * *

For the next few days, I thought about Frank, wondering with growing frustration why he hadn't called me. I missed work for a week because my sewing machine was under repair. At least it gave me an excuse to stay home, regroup, and not have to face the amusement of my colleagues at the office.

The following Monday, Ken delivered my newly repaired demo. One part of me was glad to have my beast of a machine back, but not all of me.

Later, I was in my room, sewing, when Uncle Joe knocked on my door.

"Come in," I called back.

He opened the door as I continued my work. "What are you doing?"

"Sewing." I continued hemming a skirt. *Isn't that obvious?*

He chuckled. "I guess I deserved that. What I meant to ask is, *Why* you are sewing?"

I stopped the motor. "I had a little accident a few days ago, and my demo has been in the repair shop. I'm making sure it works before I go back out to sell."

"How did your month go?"

"Not so good." I turned back to my work.

"Laura?"

I continued sewing, trying to pretend I could not hear him, hoping he would leave.

He walked closer and around to the side, until he could see my face. "Laura? How bad was it?"

"Really bad." I kept sewing.

"Remember what we say about bad?"

I sighed, finishing the hem and setting the skirt aside. "Turn the bad into good."

"Talk to me."

"I didn't even sell one solitary sewing machine. Are you happy now?"

Uncle Joe pulled a chair up to the table and sat beside me. I sniffed, determined not to cry. He got up, grabbed a handkerchief from my nightstand, and handed it to me. "Do you want to tell me what's going on?"

"Nothing is going on. That's just it! Nothing is happening! Nothing!" I blew my nose. The resulting sound was so loud that it made me laugh, and then I snorted as I tried to catch my breath. After I regained my composure, I described the trials and tribulations of my month in great detail.

Uncle Joe listened quietly, a smile playing around the corners of his mouth, and when I was done, he asked, "So, what's the problem?"

"What's the *problem*?"

Uncle Joe nodded. "Okay, let me word it differently. What have you learned?"

"It's pretty hard to sell a sewing machine when my demo is busted."

"This is true." He twisted his mustache. "Secret number one teaches us that we must dress for success, because we never get a second chance to make a first impression. Do you remember that?"

"Yes, sir, I remember."

"Do you remember secret number two?"

I sighed. "*Yes—know what you are looking for.*"

"Good. Judging by your experience this month, you need to keep working on that one. But you're learning. And while you figure out what you are looking for, having the right tools is equally important." He looked up at me and smiled. "In fact, that is secret number three: *Use The Right Tools.*"

That seemed sensible enough to me. But I already had the right tools.

"I bought a sewing machine and learned to sew," I said. "It's not my fault it broke."

"The sewing machine isn't your tool," Uncle Joe replied.

"I don't understand—"

Uncle Joe interrupted my protest. "Before I explain, let me ask you a question. Who showed you how to pan for gold?"

"My dad, of course."

"What are the steps in panning?"

"You want me to tell you?"

"Yes, tell me the steps you would go through."

"Well . . ."

I pictured myself in the river with Dad. "First, I scooped my pan into the sandy dirt and filled it about three-quarters full. Then I gently submerged the pan and soaked the contents, holding the pan horizontally. I stirred the wet material with my fingers and removed any large rocks, sticks or roots.

"Then I shook the pan left to right underwater, since that would cause the gold, which is heavy, to work its way down toward the bottom of my pan.

"Next, I stirred the water into the material and submerged my pan again, being careful to wash away any twigs, roots, rocks, or mossy material that might be in the pan with the dirt I had scooped up. Dad always said that it was a good idea to rinse any coarse, porous rocks free of any clay material stuck to their surface. The gold easily sticks to clay and can be washed downstream with the lighter rocks and gravel. Dad stressed that if I did not break apart or wash the gold out of the pores and holes in a rock before the rock passed out of my pan, I would lose some gold.

"After that, I would shake the gold pan vigorously in a small circle, mixing it up with my hand at the same time. I needed to suspend the sand, mud, rocks, and gold in water.

"Dad would always say, 'Be careful not to slosh over the sides before the gold has settled to the bottom.'"

"Continue." Uncle Joe smiled. "You're doing well."

"This gold panning step is known as stratification or layering. It creates horizontal layers of material from the various densities in the pan. The layers will have lighter rock, sand, and gravel on top and heavy black sands and gold on the bottom.

"Dad would put the pan in my hand and say, 'Now, start to tilt the pan downward while holding it just under the surface, and continue shaking it to keep the material in suspension. Stop shaking just when the material starts to slide forward. The gold will be at the lowest point in the pan right then.'"

I was enjoying the memory. This was something I knew how to do, something I was good at—unlike this crazy sales business.

"The next step is where I would shave the stratified layers out of the pan, from light to heavy. I would tip the pan to one edge just under the surface of the water, and then, while holding the pan at a 45-degree angle, pull the pan toward me. Dad would say, 'As you stop pulling, you will see a small wave pile up at the back of the pan and reflect across the sand and gravel. As the wave of water sweeps across, it will shave or sweep off a bit of layered material. Continue this action until you have removed the top layers.'

"He always warned me not to shake too much at this stage. Finally, I would swirl the gold and black sand to create a comet tail of golden colors following the black sands in my pan. That would allow me to use our gold snuffer bottle to quickly suck up the gold particles and coarse gold. Of course, I sometimes got a nugget, which I placed in our bag. I remembered how wonderful the nuggets felt, heavy and smooth and wet with river water."

"Okay," Uncle Joe said. "You were taught well. Now, let me ask you a question: which is your tool, the pan or the gold?"

"The pan."

"Correct." He leaned back. "In like manner, which is your tool, the sewing machine or your techniques for selling?"

Suddenly, I understood. I had been focused on the wrong thing.

"The sand is all the people we meet. The sifting is doing your research before you knock on the doors, then asking questions to qualify the prospects, plus keeping careful records and following through on all your leads—including, in your case, checking your messages. When someone calls asking for you specifically, that's a gold nugget! You need to get that one in the bag fast. The swirl is the ability to help the potential prospect see the gold in the midst of sand and dirt."

"Pop told you that?"

"Yep. Pop taught your dad and me not just how to prospect gold, but how to prospect people. And in both businesses, you have to be patient, thorough, and use all the right tools, if you want to be successful."

I nodded, feeling my inspiration and drive returning. Uncle Joe was right—I'd not been using the tools I'd been given. After my first month's success, I'd gotten cocky. I'd thought I could just show up on doorsteps and the sewing machines would sell themselves. And for the past week, I'd used the absence of my demo as an excuse to avoid the hard work of building relationships. Now I understood that I needed to be disciplined and strategic in my approach.

Uncle Joe's next question caught me off guard. "Now, who's this guy you met the other day?"

"What?"

"Some real estate agent, wanting to show you a house?" He grinned.

I frowned. "Ellie Mae's got a big mouth."

"So, what's he like? Tell me about him." Our prospecting lesson was clearly over for the day.

"He's a jerk!"

"What? You're interested in a jerk?" He chuckled.

"It's not funny. I gave him my number, but he hasn't called. It's been over a week now. I'm such an idiot."

"I'm sure he's got a good reason," he offered.

Sometimes I hated how positive Uncle Joe was; he could see the good in anyone or anything. He always gave people the benefit of the doubt and looked for the good in every situation, no matter how bad it looked. "Are you taking his side now?"

"No." He paused for a second and took a sip of coffee. "So what's his name?"

"Frank Roheny," I responded cautiously.

"That's Ralph's little brother." He nodded. "He's tall, well over six feet, well-dressed, and he never goes out without his shoes shined to look new."

"You know everyone in this town, don't you?"

Just then, Ellie Mae knocked on the door, then pushed it open. "Laura, you have a phone call."

"Is it Ken?"

"No, it's the *other* guy." She winked as I hurried past her into the hallway.

Frank's voice on the other end of the line was warm and reassuring. He apologized for not having called sooner, explaining that his mother had been very sick. And he invited me to dinner that week. As I happily accepted, I turned to see Uncle Joe standing in the doorway of his office, smiling from ear to ear.

* * * * *

Mrs. Collins had kindly agreed to reschedule my demonstration for Friday. I arrived promptly at three o'clock, and she introduced me to her guests, many of whom turned out to be her daughters, nieces, and granddaughters. She served finger food, cake, and fresh brewed tea. As we ate, we became more acquainted. I asked questions about each one of them, and they shared stories about their families, lives, homes, and aspirations.

Soon I became engrossed in their stories. Each mother was passionate about her children and loved being a mom. It made me think about Frank. Would he become the father of my children? Would we grow old together? *Don't be silly,* I told myself. *You don't even know him. You haven't even had dinner with him yet!* But still . . .

Mrs. Collins's granddaughter, Linda, confessed that she wanted to be a wife but wanted to pursue a career before having kids.

Her cousin, Angela, declared that Linda was selfish. Angela's mom, Joanne, corrected Angela for being contrary, despite her obvious embarrassment at having to do so, and then apologized to me for the remark.

I wasn't offended. "No, it's okay. I think it is good to discuss different opinions and ideas."

Linda attempted to clarify her earlier statement. "I'm not saying I don't want to have children, but what is wrong with wanting to have a career too? That's what Laura is doing, isn't it?"

Everyone was looking at me, waiting for my response. For the first time, I decided to open up about myself. "I think my views on women and careers are different because of my upbringing," I said. I told them how my mother had died and how my dad had raised me to become a prospector. They were wide-eyed as I described the life I'd lived, wearing men's overalls and wielding shovels, axes, and hammers as I worked beside my Dad.

When I got to the part where Dad died, I had to stop because all the women were crying, and it was distracting. I thought I should be crying too, but somehow I wasn't sad anymore. I looked around. "Ladies, don't be sad. My dad taught me to take the bad and turn it into good. I was sad when I first moved here, but now, because of the training I received from my dad and the mentoring I've had from my Uncle Joe, I am here today as a salesperson, a business capitalist, and an entrepreneur. I don't want to sell sewing machines forever. I want to own the business!"

As soon as the words came out of my mouth, I could not believe I had said that—to others, anyway. I had thought it a few times after talking with Uncle Joe, but I had never said it aloud.

"Wow, you are a dreamer," Angela gushed.

"If you don't dream, you'll have nightmares," I said. "I know which I prefer." I smiled. "I've one last thing to say, then I'll hold my tongue. If you want to find the gold, you have to go upstream. In other words, if I am going to discover my purpose, I have to pursue my dreams with all my might. I must fight against the obstacles, distractions, disappointments, and detours. I can never give up!"

To my surprise, all the women around the living room began to applaud, getting to their feet. I was embarrassed, so I tried to wave them into silence. Until that moment, I hadn't realized how much the book of secrets and Uncle Joe's teaching had changed me. I was actually becoming a prospector.

As the applause died down, Jackie proclaimed, "You need to write a book!" The others agreed.

I just laughed as the women reseated themselves. "I may write a book someday, but today I want to show you the Red Eye 66."

I sold five sewing machines that day, and each of the women gave me a list of family members and friends, who might be interested. My prospect list grew by eighty-three names in less than three hours. Most importantly, I'd discovered one of my most powerful tools: my own story.

I practically skipped down the driveway to my car, the warm goodbyes of the women echoing in my ears. The afternoon had passed so quickly, and they felt like old friends. And then I realized it was after five o'clock. I was already late for my dinner with Frank!

10

Get Back in the River

I DROVE FASTER THAN I probably should have, but even so, I was forty minutes late. I hurried into the restaurant, gave Frank's name to the host, and was escorted to the dining area. There he was, seated at a table alone, a glass of wine and a half-eaten salad before him. *He had started without me!* Suddenly I was more irritated than embarrassed.

When he saw me, he smiled, dabbed his face with a napkin, stood up, and walked around the table to hold out my chair for me. "I thought you stood me up."

I tried to explain. "I made sixty-five dollars in commissions in three hours—"

What am I doing? Don't talk about yourself! Make it about him!

"How much did you make today?" I asked.

Wow, nice way to put him on the spot, Laura.

He sat down opposite me, chuckling. "She's sassy too. I like that."

I thought he was making fun of me. "You have no idea," I snapped.

When the waiter came and asked me what I wanted to drink, Frank suggested a wine I might like.

"I'll have whatever beer is on tap." I snatched up a menu and ignored him.

He must have realized that I was upset, even if he didn't know why. He asked about my day, and I reluctantly shared about the meeting at Mrs. Collins's home.

He seemed genuinely excited by my success. Soon I found myself relaxing, telling him other stories from my short career in sales. He laughed at the baseball incident and then backpedaled under the heat of my glare. He commiserated with my horrible first day. When I mentioned my failed attempts to sell in Germantown, he covered his mouth, attempting to hide his mirth to avoid my wrath. But as a grin spread across my face, he relaxed, allowing his laugh to echo through the restaurant.

It was obvious that Frank was not disapproving of or intimidated by my zeal to be a businesswoman. In fact, he said that my independence was what had convinced him to call me. He was the first man I had met, besides Uncle Joe and Ken, who seemed to believe that a woman has the right to pursue a career, or even to own her own business.

When we finished dinner, it was late—almost 10:30 p.m. He walked me to my car, thanked me for a great evening, and asked if we could have dinner on Sunday, to which I happily agreed. I stood at my car door, dangling my keys, and lowered my head, wondering what was next. Frank was a gentleman in every way, and when he said, "Good night," I looked up. With no hesitation, he leaned forward, I responded, and we kissed.

* * * * *

The following week, I started making calls to schedule appointments with my new prospects. I couldn't believe that I had eighty-three names. Mrs. Collins's daughters and granddaughters had given me very positive reviews, and their friends seemed eager to demand the privilege of hosting my demonstrations. Mrs. Collins offered to hold meetings in her home so I could demonstrate the machine to several women at once. At each meeting I used my newly discovered tool, sharing a ten-minute version of my own story.

The results were astounding! I did four demonstrations that month, with seven to ten women present each time, not counting Mrs. Collins and her family. Jackie, Linda, Angela, and Joanne often showed up to help out and serve snacks and tea. I sold forty-seven sewing machines that month, and my prospect list grew to over two hundred and fifty names. The following month, I had three meetings, sold fifty-seven sewing machines, and saw my prospect list grow to three hundred and seventy-six names.

Jackie, Joanne, Linda, and Angela became my indispensable partners, and I started paying them a small share of my commissions in return for their help with the demonstrations. It wasn't much, but none of them had earned their own money before, and I loved seeing the pride in their faces and the feeling of independence it gave them. Mrs. Collins refused to accept any payment, insisting that her life was so much more interesting since she had met me, so I had to content myself with bringing her gifts for her home.

I was excited by my success, but I was also exhausted. Frank was patient with me, but I was still showing up late for dinner dates, and I had to cancel three times. One of those times, I later found out, he had been planning to surprise me with tickets to the opera.

One night, after our last meeting for the month, Jackie sat down beside me as I was packing up the Singer. "Girl, you look terrible," she said.

"Thanks!"

"No. Really." Jackie frowned. "You look tired. Are you getting enough sleep?"

"Well, not really," I admitted. "The paperwork for all these sales is becoming almost overwhelming."

By this time, all the guests had gone, and Mrs. Collins, Jackie, Joanne, Linda, and Angela gathered round with cups of tea. These women had become my valued friends, and I couldn't possibly have achieved what I had without their generosity and support.

Angela smiled mischievously. "How are things going with Frank?"

Joanne frowned. "Angela, that's not something you ask." She turned to me. "You don't have to answer that."

I didn't mind. In fact, it was good to have people to talk to. "Well, actually, now that you mention it, not so great. I work so much that we hardly get to see each other."

"Girl!" Mrs. Collins interjected. "You've got to close the deal!"

Everyone laughed.

"Do you love him?" Angela burst in.

"You know, I think I do," I replied, almost surprising myself.

Frank was the opposite of me in many ways—sophisticated, romantic, polite, patient, and always impeccably dressed. He would leave me little love notes tucked under the wipers on my windshield so I'd find them in the morning. He always treated me like a lady, opening doors for me and insisting on carrying my bags. And yet he respected my independence and never talked down to me. The more time I spent with him, the more I wanted to be with him.

"Then what are you waiting for?" Angela demanded. "Marry the guy!"

Everyone nodded enthusiastic agreement.

I looked down at my feet. "It's not that easy. I hardly even see him these days because my job takes so much of my time. How can I know if I'm ready to marry someone if I can't even find time to have dinner with him?"

"It sounds like your job is a distraction," Joanne noted.

Mrs. Collins patted my arm. "You need to slow down, girl."

Joanne nodded. Then her expression brightened. "I have an idea! Why don't we meet just once or twice a month? We can invite more guests but meet less often. That way, you can spend more time with Frank and find out if he's the one or not."

I shook my head. "I don't know. I can't afford to let my numbers drop now that I have momentum."

"But if you don't slow down, you might end up an old maid, like Miss Cunningham down the street!" Angela warned, ignoring her mother's disapproving glance.

Finally, I agreed. "Let's continue with three meetings per month for the next two months, but for the third month, we'll cut back to two and see how that works. What do you think?"

I appreciated the sympathy of my friends, but a nagging voice in the back of my mind wondered what Uncle Joe would think about me taking advice from housewives on how to run my business. But what did he know about balancing a career and a romance? He wasn't a woman. So I didn't tell him my plans. I did tell Frank that I was planning to work less after a couple more months so that we could spend more time together, and he was not opposed to the idea. However, he wanted to be sure that it was what I wanted, not what others wanted for me. I assured him it was.

For the next two months, I threw myself into selling sewing machines. In the first month, we had sixty-nine new people attend the demonstrations and netted fifty-three sales. The second month, ninety-nine people attended, and I sold seventy sewing machines—the most by a single salesperson in one month in the history of the company. I had only been selling sewing machines for six months, and for five of those months, I was my company's top salesperson in the state. By the sixth month, I was the number one Singer salesperson in the United States. I had learned how to use the right tools and the results were beyond what I could have imagined! Now that I'd gotten my momentum established, surely I could afford to focus on Frank for a while.

* * * * *

Frank made big plans for our first full Saturday together. He took me to White City Amusement Park, on the corner of 63rd and Cottage Grove, to see the "City of a Million Electric Lights." I'd never been to an amusement park before, and I loved it. Two weeks later, he took me to another one, the Riverview Amusement Park on North Western Avenue, which had over a hundred and fifty-six acres of attractions. We rode Ferris wheels, rollercoasters, and a seventy-horse carousel, and viewed ostriches, crocodiles, and a reenactment of Indian fights.

The next weekend, we went to Vaudeville for a live show and toured Polyscope, the world's first movie studio, where Charlie Chaplin made his films. Several nights a week, we talked for hours over delicious dinners at the Blackhawk nightclub, Friar's Inn, or our favorite spot, the Southside Café, where jazz singers and musicians filled the air with rhythms that begged us to dance. We heard stars such as Alberta Hunter, Ethel Waters, Louis Armstrong, and clarinetist Jimmie Noone.

I thoroughly enjoyed every moment we were now able to spend together. I was more convinced every day that he was the man I wanted to marry, but I feared that I could not live up to his expectations. I felt like he had only seen me during the good times, when my business was booming and I was winning awards. But how long would it last? The pattern of my life was like the rollercoasters at Riverview Amusement Park—up and down. My greatest fear was that I would eventually crash, and that when I did, Frank would desert me.

* * * * *

As my first year at Singer drew to a close, my absence from the sales office was beginning to frustrate Ken. He grew tired of me calling off or rescheduling appointments and not returning calls. In fact, he told me that if I hadn't been the top salesperson in the company, he would have fired me months ago. I didn't care; I was invincible. Around that time, Frank brokered a deal for a business owner, Thomas Turner, who opened a hat-cleaning shop on the main floor of a massive new building called the Pioneer Arcade, located on the West Side of Chicago. The *Tribune* called it "one of the city's finest and most elaborate recreational buildings."

I was in awe of its beauty and splendor on my first visit. The entrance was decorated to resemble a seventeenth-century Spanish palace, adorned with elaborate carvings and triple arches around the doors. The ceilings were lined with intricately detailed beams, and the lobby was all but filled by a wide, Baroque-inspired, double-flight staircase that was the primary path for guests.

The Pioneer Arcade had been created to become *the* place in Chicago for pleasure and entertainment. It housed thirty-five billiard tables and a bowling alley with twenty lanes that could be viewed from a gallery on the mezzanine level. Frank and I went back there often. And I loved to bowl, even though I was not very good at it.

One afternoon, Frank asked me to go with him to go visit Thomas Turner, the owner of the hat-cleaning shop, to see how things were going and to discuss the possibility of a second location in a building he was selling across town.

The hat-cleaning shop was crammed in with three other retail stores: a cigar vendor, the Arcade Lunch Room and, oddly, a Singer Sewing Machine sales and repair shop. The owner of this last was an independent dealer, and according to Frank, he had health problems; the store was closed more than it was open. In fact, Frank confessed, his desire for me to see the Singer shop was the real reason he had wanted me to come with him that day. He promised to explain after we'd finished his other business.

However, we never made it to the Singer store. After we entered the Top Hat Cleaning Shop, Frank and Mr. Turner visited for a brief moment, and then Frank introduced me.

"Thomas, this is my girl, Laura." Frank always made it a point to tell people of my success. He was so proud of my achievements. "Laura is the top salesperson for the Singer Sewing Company."

"Oh, really? What regional office do you work out of?"

I smiled. "The East Side."

Thomas frowned. "So you're the one!"

"Excuse me?" I asked, sensing an abrupt change in his mood but not understanding why.

Frank could feel the conversation deteriorating, so he interjected, "Well, I have to get Laura back to work. I'll catch up with you another time, Thomas." He grabbed my elbow and attempted to escort me out.

Feeling I was being "handled," I jerked my arm out of Frank's hand, spun about, and glared at Thomas. "You got something you want to say?" I asked him.

Frank rested his hand on my shoulder. "Come on. Let's go, honey."

I held up a finger. "One second, Frank. Thomas was about to explain."

"You're the one who crippled Mr. Martin's business, which drove him into bad health."

"Who? I did what?"

"Mr. Martin owns the sewing machine repair shop next door. He said that in the last year, his business has collapsed because some hotshot woman came in and changed all the rules by meeting in homes and recruiting other women to do the work with promises of profitable returns. Sounds like what that Charles Ponzi did. And if you are the top salesperson at Singer, I'm guessing that would be you. Do you realize what you've done? He has heart problems and is losing his business because of you!" Thomas marched back behind the counter, mumbling, "Besides, sales is a man's job."

Excuse me? Now he had crossed a line. "If sales is a 'man's job,' what does it say that I'm the best in the *country*? Is every man in the nation less of a man than me?" I glared at him. "If you have a problem, let's settle it salesperson to salesperson—"

"Laura!" Frank attempted to take my arm again, but this just fueled my rage.

I spun on him. "No, Frank. It's men like this who are holding women back, denying them their rights. This is America, for God's sake. If women can vote, then they can run or own their own businesses!"

I turned back to the shop owner. "Let me tell you something, buddy. I have worked hard for everything I have, and no one handed it to me. If your friend is sick, I wish him a speedy recovery. But if he's losing his business because he can't sell a sewing machine, then maybe he should let a woman do it!"

With that, I walked out. Frank tried to calm me down and convince me to let it go, but the incident dredged up too many feelings and memories—men whistling at me, holding me back, and keeping me from success.

Frank knew how I felt about women's rights. He knew I'd volunteered with the League of Women Voters organization that supported the passage of the Nineteenth Amendment in 1920. I'd vowed to change the system and prove that women were not just homemakers.

Now I decided I was going to teach the hat cleaner a lesson. I met with a group of women at Mrs. Collins's home, and they agreed that this man needed to be put in his place. We organized a protest and marched in front of his store. Unfortunately, we didn't know that we needed a permit to picket, so when Thomas called the police, we were told that we would have to move on.

I immediately applied for the permit, but a response was slow in coming. While we waited, I called another meeting of my group. We picketed other business owners who were opposed to women's equality, and on two occasions I gave speeches as to why women should have the right to own their own businesses. Two weeks later, I received a denial letter from the city commissioner's office that prevented us from picketing Top Hat. Incensed, I called my fledgling women's rights group together yet again, and this time we vowed to organize our efforts and fight City Hall.

* * * * *

In the midst of one of our impassioned meetings in Mrs. Collins's kitchen, the phone rang. It was Ken, looking for me. I had not been in the office for more than three weeks, so getting a call from Ken was highly unusual. My heart raced as I walked to the hallway to take the call.

"Laura, it's Ken."

"Is everything all right?"

"I guess so. Well, I don't know—"

"What is it then?"

"Your uncle, Mr. Dunagan, called and asked me to track you down and inform you that he needs to speak with you right away. *Is* everything all right?"

I assured Ken that all was well and that he shouldn't worry. Then, after explaining to the ladies that an urgent matter had come up, I shot out the door and down the road, my mind flying in a million directions. *Is it Matthew? Is it Frank? Is Uncle Joe all right? Is it Ellie Mae? I lost my mom, and then my dad. Who could it be this time?*

I pulled into the circular drive of the mansion, left my car outside the front door, and ran inside. The first person I saw was Ellie Mae. I embraced her, relieved. "You're all right!"

Ellie Mae was clearly confused, which added to my relief. Evidently she didn't know of any tragedy.

"Happy to see you too," she shouted after me as I let her go and ran off down the hallway. As I passed the dining room, I saw Aunt Debra tending to some flowers on the table. I waved and continued down the hall.

Without pausing to knock, I burst into the office. "Uncle Joe, is everything all right?"

"That's what I'm trying to find out."

I let out a huge sigh. There hadn't been a death or injury in the family. My relief, however, was short-lived. I began to mentally list the reasons he might want to talk to me: *the picketing, my rude comments to the Top Hat owner, my absence from work, or the fact that I had not been in his office for over three months.*

Uncle Joe was holding a magazine in his hand. He held it up so I could see the cover. In large letters it read, *TIME: The Weekly News-Magazine*. The upper right-hand corner announced the price, "15 cents." The cover showed a picture of a beautiful woman, labeled "Eleanora Duse." I recognized her face from the posters outside the movie theater.

Uncle Joe nodded toward a framed picture of me that was sitting on a table beneath the window. "Someday, I believe your picture will be on this cover, and it will read, *The Greatest Prospector In The World*," he said. He placed the magazine on the table and looked me straight in the eye. "But if that's to happen, I need you to explain to me what's going on."

Before I could answer, he continued, "A few weeks ago, Frank contacted me about a Singer sales and repair shop in the Pioneer Arcade. He said it might be coming available soon. He wanted to know how well I knew the owner, and if I would make some calls. He wanted to surprise you with it, but some things have come to light during my investigations and negotiations, and I would like to discuss them with you."

I was not sure what he wanted to discuss with me, but somehow Uncle Joe could still intimidate me, even then. My heart raced and my palms sweated.

"I decided to call a friend in New York, who is the vice president of Singer, to talk about you buying out that franchise. First, before we would offer a bid on the storefront, I needed to see if there were nondisclosure agreements, conflicts of interest, or other legal issues that might prohibit you from opening your own sewing machine company. According to my friend, there are no legal concerns with Singer and a buyout is a possibility. The negotiations would be with the independent dealer, not with the corporate office in New York City.

"Then I called the owner of the Pioneer Arcade, Carl Jorgensen, known as Jorgy. He is a liberal, so he has no conflict with women's rights and no objections to a woman owning her own business. However, not everyone feels the way he and I do. So, Jorgy wanted to see some sales numbers first, before he would sell the property to a woman. If he is to risk his reputation, he wants to be sure the person, in this case you, has the capital and experience to make it work. Businesses come and go every day. Jorgy said he doesn't mind being associated with a female-owned business, but he does *not* want to be associated with a bankrupt, female-owned business."

Uncle Joe paused in his story and looked at me. "Laura, do you know how many women in Chicago own their own businesses right now?"

"No, sir."

"Very few. And those who do are generally in the hospitality industries, like restaurants or hotels. You could make history by being one of the first, if not *the* first, to own a commercial sales business."

"So what's the problem?"

"The problem is your sales reports. I had Ken send them to me, and when I read them over, I saw that your last three months have plummeted. What's going on?"

"Nothing's going on. I mean, I have been busy these past few months, but I made my annual sales quota over five months ago. So what's the problem?"

"For the past six months, you have declined in sales, sales projections, and prospect names. In the past two months, you have sold only twenty-one sewing machines. You sold that many in your first two weeks. What have you been doing?"

I rolled my eyes. "Living my life, Uncle Joe."

"What, specifically, have you accomplished toward your ultimate goal?"

"What goal?"

"Becoming the greatest prospector in the world!"

"I needed some time for myself. I was afraid I might lose Frank, so I backed off from the business and spent more time with him."

"I thought you told me he had no problem with you building your business. When I spoke with Frank about these sales numbers, he was surprised. He said you told him your business was running itself and that you had some women helping you. He had no idea you'd stopped selling! And what about the past two months? Are these numbers a result of the picketing?"

I cringed. "Oh, then you heard about that," I said. Nothing went on in Chicago that Uncle Joe did not know about. His connections were endless.

"Heard about it?" He shook his head. "The mayor called me to ask if you were my daughter, wanting to know if I could do something about it."

"It's just wrong, Uncle Joe, how men are treating women these days!"

"I understand that and I agree. But, Laura, you've got to prioritize your time, efforts, work habits, and actions based on your goals. Anything that you do or that happens to you that is *not* a part of reaching your goals is a distraction!"

When he said that, I remembered the day the ladies encouraged me to prioritize Frank over my job. As clear as a bell, I could hear Angela's words: *Your job is a distraction!*

"Laura, if your goal in life is to be an activist, then so be it. If your goal is to be Frank's wife and build a family, you have my blessing. But all your life, all the years you've been with me, you have never detoured from one thing: your desire to become *The Greatest Prospector In The World.*" He paused for a moment before continuing.

"Let me ask you. Has that dream died? Do you no longer want it?"

He didn't wait for me to answer. I knew Uncle Joe well enough by now to know when he had something to teach me, so I kept quiet and listened.

"Allow me to share a story," he said. "When my father moved to Alaska, he made it clear to your Dad and me that the money he'd inherited from Papa James was gone. He had spent his last bit of savings on supplies, equipment, and our boat tickets. When the Klondike Gold Rush hit, there were no bountiful provisions of gold lying around, visible to all. Thousands traveled to strike it rich, and most returned empty-handed. Moving to Alaska was our last-ditch effort to make it. If we did not find gold, we would be penniless. For Pop, panning for gold was not an option—it was all or nothing. We had to make it work. Our mission was to find gold, and we could not stop until we reached our goal."

As Uncle Joe told his story, my mind drifted back to the cabin. I relaxed a little. I could envision myself sitting on the floor with my arm on dad's knee, he in his favorite chair near the potbelly stove. Dad had told me this same story dozens of times, but now, when Uncle Joe retold it, I finally understood.

The first time Dad told me this story, we'd had a rough day in the river. It was cold, and it had rained all day. I was soaked. More than once, I had begged Dad to quit and go back to the cabin. But the more it rained, the harder he worked. It drove me crazy. He just would not stop. I was tired, cold, wet, and exhausted, and I was definitely ready to stop for the day, but he would not quit. We had already found gold that day, so I could not understand why he kept working.

I pouted and refused to talk to him all the way back to the cabin. That night, as I watched Dad add wood to the stove, I was still angry. I had made up my mind I was not going to speak to him. That night, I wanted to quit and never go back to the river.

Just then, Dad turned around, saw that I was mad, and started to laugh. I asked him what was so funny. Instead of giving me a simple, short answer, he told me this same story about prospecting with his father, Pop Angus.

Dad told me that on many days, he had wanted to quit or stop early because of bad weather conditions or fatigue. One day, he was exhausted, but they had not found any gold. Standing on the bank, ready to pack his tools, Dad begged his father to quit early. Nevertheless, Pop Angus would remind him why they were there. They were there to find gold—at least two ounces per day—and they were not going to stop until they reached their goal.

Pop Angus asked my dad, "Have we reached our daily goal yet, son?"

"No."

"Then get back into the river!"

I was so caught up in my recollection of my dad's story that I forgot, for a moment, where I was.

"Laura. Laura!" Uncle Joe was calling me, as if to wake me up from a dream. "Laura, pay attention, I'm trying to talk to you!"

Having regained my attention, he said, "If you want to do well in this business, you need to get back into the river! You need to  get back to building your business. If you still want to become the greatest prospector in the world, you need to set some priorities, boundaries, and guidelines, so that you will not get derailed by distractions.

"You need to ask yourself: what is your desire, what outcome do you want, and *why* do you want it? Why? Why? Why? That's the most important question. Why are you doing what you are doing? It is because you have a dream, a destiny, a plan, a goal? But you will never, never reach your dream, if you get out of the water before you are done.

"Your fear of losing Frank was a distraction. Your inability to control your temper with the hat shop owner was a distraction. Both of these distractions pulled you away from building your business and caused you to forget what your mission is. You need to get back into the river! Distractions are like the cold weather, bitter winters, and poor conditions in Alaska. When you know *why* you are doing what you are doing, and you know what your goals are, you won't stop! You will stay in the river until you reach your target.

"Laura, you cannot be satisfied with achieving the company's annual quota. Those numbers, which help you be considered for a raise or a promotion, are for average people. You are not average! You are not even just above average. You are over the top! To be the best, you need to set an annual projection that exceeds your quota. Once you have that number, you will know what your monthly projections are.

"As for this picketing thing—I know how passionate you feel about this topic. I have not forgotten how mistreated you were at the Chicago Mercantile and the *Tribune*. I believe Mr. Turner was insensitive and offensive—he mouths off to a lot of people. But Laura, you know that the passing of the Nineteenth Amendment gave women the right to vote, but did not eliminate narrow-minded thinking. Men like him will always be around. You don't picket a business because you don't like a man or his personal views. To be an activist for equal rights is a worthy and notable act. But the time you are wasting on this fool of a man is ridiculous!"

I hung my head, embarrassed. He was right.

"You need to sit down and write out life goals. You need to see yourself in the future: in one year, five years, ten years. What do you see yourself doing or becoming? Then, you set small goals and spread them out over a span of time. That will get you to your final destination.

"It's not enough to set just any goal; a goal should be a tangible idea that stretches you. A goal must have a date or a deadline, because a goal without a date is just a fantasy. In other words, it is not enough just to get into the river and pan for gold—you need to know how much you intend to find, and by when. Otherwise, you will get out of the river when it's too cold, when it's raining, when you're tired, when you're hungry, or when your emotions long for something else—and that something else, at the time, might seem harmless or good. But if it does not take you to your desired future, it will lead you astray. Many good prospectors have walked away from the prize because they got distracted. Laura, get back into the river!"

I sat there, frozen to the spot by the force of his words.

"When we finish talking, I want you to go somewhere to focus and write down your goals," he said. "Then, as soon as possible, meet with Frank and set goals with him. Come to an agreement on how much time you will spend together to reach whatever goals you set for your relationship. The way Frank talks about you tells me that he loves you. If he loves you, he will support you and help you get where you want to go.

When you have your goals written down, ask yourself—is what I have been doing in the past six months helping me reach my goals? If not, something needs to be eliminated, scaled back, or brought into balance. Are you getting this?"

"I am."

"So now you know … " He paused, mid-sentence.

I waited to see if he was going to finish the thought, but he seemed to be finished.

"Uncle Joe, now I know what?"

"Oh—now you know secret number four: *Get Into The River, Even When You Don't Want To.*"

The fourth secret. How had I waited so long to learn this next lesson? I closed my eyes, my mind flashing over all the things I'd been doing these past months—the amusement parks, the dinners, the picketing, the women's rights meetings—and I could hear Dad's voice echoing through all of it: "Get back into the river!" How had I not heard him?

* * * * *

I did exactly what Uncle Joe recommended. I went up to my bedroom, sat down at my sewing table, and took out my notebook. I visualized myself in the future, and the first words that came to me were: *I want to mentor a special person toward becoming The Greatest Prospector In The World.* That surprised me, but I wrote it down.

For the next three hours, I wrote down goals, set dates, and made decisions about what to change in my schedule to match my goals. The first thing I decided was to put an end to the picketing. I also resolved to meet with Frank and discuss our future. When I completed my list, I had twenty-two pages penned.

I closed the notebook and stared at it for a few seconds. My vision blurred, and for a moment the covers seemed to age and darken, and I could see the handwritten title that Pop Angus had penned, *The Greatest Prospector In The World.*

I reached out and ran my fingertips across the ink that Pop Angus used to emboss the title on the leather-bound manuscript. Slowly, I lifted the cover, but as I did so, the vision faded and the book in my hand was my own notebook, new and shiny. I opened it fully, and I saw:

I want to mentor a special person toward becoming The Greatest Prospector In The World.

11

That's Hilarious!

BEFORE FRANK AND I SET our goals together, he wanted to know mine. That way, our schedule and plans could coincide. When I told him I had twenty-two pages, he laughed.

"What's so funny?" I asked, feigning hurt feelings.

"Nothing, dear."

"Yeah, right," I replied.

"Still as sassy as you were on our first date." He smiled, enjoying the memory.

"You wouldn't have it any other way."

I opened the notebook, looked down, and saw my first goal, which I had penned the night before. I turned the page, hoping he wouldn't notice. I was not ready for Frank to see that yet. It was too personal.

"What was that?"

"Nothing."

Frank knew me well enough not to push, so he left it alone.

We went through my list of goals, one-by-one. When we came to *Increase my prospect list*, Frank said, "How many names do you currently have on your prospect list?"

"Over one hundred."

"And how many do you want by this time next year?"

"At least five hundred."

He nodded to himself. "You need a thousand."

"What?" I realized I had shouted, and lowered my voice. "A thousand? That's impossible!"

"Hear me out. When you had your first meeting at Mrs. Collins's home, how many women were there?"

"Six."

"And how many referrals did you get from that meeting?"

"Eighty-three."

"All right, let us suppose you host a meeting with twelve women and you get a hundred names. If you do that ten times, then you have a thousand new referrals on your prospect list. Even if you get only fifty names per meeting, hosting twenty meetings will get you to a thousand names."

We continued to go over the goals and came to the one that said, *Own my own business*. Frank became excited. He started to tell me about the possibility of purchasing the storefront in the Pioneer Arcade. I thought about my meeting with Uncle Joe the night before.

"Frank, what if Jorgy says no?"

"Why would he say no, Laura?" Frank asked.

"Uncle Joe said that my sales numbers for the past two months were too low."

"Don't worry about that right now. The current owner of the sewing machine shop told me that if I could hold off on a buyer for six months, that that would help him greatly. He wants to show it as a loss on his taxes. It will take a couple of months for due diligence, negotiations, inspections, appraisal, and closing. That gives us eight months for you to increase your numbers before we submit an offer for the shop. By then, everything will be in order and Jorgy will be fine. Besides, Uncle Joe is backing you, and he knows Jorgy real well."

"Yeah, I guess you're right."

* * * * *

I went right to work on my goals. The first thing I did was to attach the individual months of a large calendar to the wall in my office. I marked each goal on its projected date, creating a visual representation of my tangible goals and reachable deadlines.

Next, I met with my women's group at Mrs. Collins's house. I shared my goals with them, and when I told them about wanting to start my own business, they were so happy and excited for me. They wanted to know where I would open my store, but I had to tell them that it was still confidential.

We went over the calendar and set dates for demonstrations. My little team had grown. My old friend Sandy from the *Tribune* had joined, along with a couple of friends of Angela's and Linda's. They were all excited about the opportunity to earn a little money and work together. We compiled a strategy to be better equipped. I was to focus on sales, and they would help with getting referrals, taking orders, building relationships with the new customers, and making follow-up calls.

Mrs. Patterson, my first sale, had also joined us, and she declared that she wanted to organize meetings at her house as well and invite the women from her church. I was speechless.

We had a plan, and we dove into action to complete it. At times, it was hectic and stressful, but the bond we women built during the next six months was amazing. What was more astounding, however, was the help we received from their husbands. Even Frank came to many of the meetings, and the men would stand on the front porch at Mrs. Collins's house and in the greenhouse in back of Mrs. Patterson's home.

The first month was a challenge, ironing out the details and training the girls to do the paperwork. Company policy prohibited other people from filling out the forms, but the only way I could double my sales in a short period was for them to gather all the information, then have me sign it.

Another action I took, which I hadn't considered before, was to purchase ten Red Eye 66s with my own money so that my customers wouldn't have to wait ten to fourteen days to get their Singer. I wanted to build excitement and generate enthusiasm, which would produce better results with referrals. It worked. At the second meeting, twelve women placed orders, but I only had those ten new sewing machines with me. The remaining two women were happy to wait, but even so, I filled their orders myself, as quickly as I could.

The following day, I purchased twenty sewing machines. Somehow, I even talked Matthew into helping with the meetings. At first, he opposed the idea, but when I offered to pay him, he agreed. Once Matthew started coming and hanging out with the guys, he enjoyed it so much that he didn't even want my money anymore. The men would gather around the radio and listen to baseball games and other sporting events.

I wanted to sell at least a hundred sewing machines each month, but by the third month, I was beating that goal by sixty percent.

* * * * *

It had been six months since I "got back into the river," and I had already broken every sales record Singer tracked. The vice president of the company even came to Chicago to meet me. Of course, he visited Uncle Joe as well, and they attended a Cubs game.

Frank was busy compiling the paperwork for negotiations with Mr. Martin, the owner of the West Side Singer Sales and Repair, as well as with Jorgy.

When Frank and Uncle Joe reviewed the sales reports, Uncle Joe was floored. He couldn't understand how I had accomplished the dramatic change. Frank explained my system to him. In the end, Uncle Joe came up with several ideas to expand my business even further.

First, he was of the opinion that I should go independent, and start my own business instead of a franchise. He recommended "Dunagan Textiles" as the name. Second, he suggested that I offer the women I was currently working with not just a percentage of my commissions, but an opportunity to start their own home businesses, selling sewing machines. I would do the training, and they would use the techniques I developed. Third, he recommended that each person who started one of the home businesses receive commissions for sales and additional bonuses for recruiting other women to start businesses from their homes. He explained that he had come up with the idea of these micro-businesses because they were smaller and less expensive.

Finally, he advised me to install a room in the storefront that would contain a number of ready-to-use sewing machines. There we could perform demonstrations, train new sales people, and start a seamstress club where women could share ideas and develop relationships. This would develop new leads and sales opportunities in a relaxed atmosphere.

Frank thought it was brilliant, but I was overwhelmed. I only knew how to build relationships and sell sewing machines, not run a business or develop micro-businesses for others. However, when I thought further, I could see myself continuing to do what I was doing while also passing it down to other women. I considered it an opportunity to help remove the barriers that hindered women from becoming entrepreneurs.

Uncle Joe calmed my nerves when he said that these business ideas could develop in stages. First, I would establish my own business. I would then implement the others over time.

Frank finished the negotiations for the storefront with Jorgy, and he found another buyer for Mr. Martin's sewing sales and repair franchise. Instead, I started Dunagan Textiles.

* * * * *

It took two months to remodel the storefront. Uncle Joe provided me with various pictures of him, Dad, and Pop Angus to display for easy viewing and remind me of the prospecting days in Alaska. They were quite the talking piece and would give me opportunities to share the story of where I came from.

We scheduled a ribbon-cutting ceremony for the grand opening. Uncle Joe made a big deal about it, and word got out: this would be the first female-owned, commercial sales business in Chicago! This news even made it to the business section of the *Chicago Tribune*! I imagined my old bosses' chagrin as they were forced to advertise *my* success. Payback, indeed.

On opening day, we all stood out front: Frank and I, Uncle Joe, Aunt Debra and Matthew, Ellie Mae and Mr. Robinson, and my women's group too. Frank and I took the giant scissors and cut the ribbon. The flash of cameras lit up the sidewalk as we stepped into the new store. Cheers and applause thundered for the grand occasion.

We had refreshments to celebrate, and we were joined by dignitaries, members of the mayor's office, and the county commissioner. Jorgy provided a live jazz band for entertainment, and we gave everyone a spool of thread with our company name printed on it. Even Ken Dawson, my former manager from Singer, showed up. He told me I deserved this success and that he had always known this day would come.

When the crowd had subsided and only close friends and family remained, we passed out champagne glasses, and Uncle Joe tapped his, sending a ringing tone through the shop.

"I want to make a toast to an incredible person," he announced. Then he grinned. "Yes, I know I'm biased, because she's my niece. To many of you, she is a comrade, a confidant, a businesswoman, a top salesperson, and an unpredictable girl—"

"That's for sure," Ellie Mae called out, and laughter rippled through the group.

"But to me ... " Uncle Joe started, then paused for a moment as tears began to fill his eyes. "To me, she is the greatest prospector in the world!" With that, Uncle Joe lifted his glass high. "To Laura!" he exclaimed.

The others lifted their glasses high and shouted in unison, "To Laura!"

Then Uncle Joe asked everyone to wait a moment, because Frank had an announcement to make. I thought he was going to say something about the company or announce what the store hours were. Instead, he reached into his pocket and pulled out a small, velvet box, opening it as he fell to one knee.

"Laura Dunagan, will you marry me?" he asked.

It was a dazzling white, six-carat diamond ring. I placed both my hands over my mouth, gasped for air, and started crying. The women were still teary-eyed from Uncle Joe's toast, and now they were laughing from joy and surprise.

It grew quiet as everyone waited for my answer. After a long moment, Matthew spoke out. "Well, what do you say? Don't keep him waiting, Laura!"

Everyone laughed, and that was a good thing, because all I could think was, *Shut up, Matthew!*

Frank stared upward as I gazed down at him and answered, "On one condition."

Uncle Joe chuckled. "Be careful now, Frank, she knows how to strike a bargain."

Frank ignored the laughter. "What is it?"

"Shave your mustache, and don't grow it back."

Frank had been clean-shaven when we met, but he had grown a mustache while we were remodeling the storefront. I hated it. I had asked him several times to shave it, because it interfered with our kisses. However, he had refused. Now I had him trapped, with a captivated audience on my side.

"I will shave it for you," he responded.

"Then I'll marry you!"

Frank stood up, reached for my hand, and placed the ring on my finger.

"Wrong hand!" Mrs. Patterson shouted out. "You got the wrong hand!"

It was as much my fault as Frank's. I switched hands as my cheeks grew warm, and he slipped the ring on my finger. I held it up to my face to get a better look at it as all the women gathered around, giggling, gawking, and commenting on its splendor.

We celebrated for another hour before people began to trickle away. Finally, only Frank, Matthew, Uncle Joe, and I remained. Frank and Matthew stood out front, talking business and real estate, while Uncle Joe and I walked to the back area, inspecting the final touches. Exhausted from the days leading up to the opening, I sat down, took off my shoes, and started rubbing my feet. Uncle Joe, with his usual cup of black coffee in hand, sat down next to me.

"You've come a long way, girl." He placed a hand on my shoulder. "I'm proud of you."

"Thank you." I sighed, suddenly aware of how exhausted I was.

"It's hard to believe this is the same girl who arrived in Chicago in waders, overalls, and her Dad's hat, angry at the whole world."

I smiled at the memory.

"But here we are." He cleared his throat. "Starting your own business comes with a lot of challenges, responsibilities, and heartache. There will be days when you will want to pull your hair out, lose your temper, and fire the next person who walks into your office. There will be times when you will ask yourself, Why am I doing this? But remember what I taught you about the 'whys' in life. Your 'why' will define you. It will give you the grit and fortitude to fight through every distraction, obstacle, and disappointing day. And trust me, they will come. Pop Angus always said, 'Your why should make you cry.'

"But there is another important secret to overcoming," he continued. "You know what it is, Laura?"

"Having a lot of money?" I offered with a smile.

Uncle Joe laughed. "Well, I suppose that doesn't hurt, but that is not what you need to survive hard times and difficult days.

Here is the secret: Learn to laugh." He grinned. "That's what Pop Angus taught me and your dad. No matter how hard you work, if you don't learn to laugh, you'll grow weary and go crazy!"

Uncle Joe leaned back, and I could tell a story was brewing. Sure enough, he said, "One time, back in Alaska, I was moving some rocks to pan the sandy dirt in the river when I found a crawdad. When Billy—your dad—wasn't paying attention, I dropped that crawdad down the back of his waders. It started biting him on the butt, and he dropped to the ground and rolled about, slapping himself on the rear end and trying to make the crawdad let him go."

I laughed aloud. "Are you kidding me?"

"Nope," he said, grinning.

I laughed so hard that I started choking, which, of course, started me hiccupping. I had to get a glass of water. When I returned, I was still giggling, the occasional hiccup providing a nice counterpoint.

"What's so funny?" he asked when I came back.

"I've never heard you say the word *butt* before. And the fact that you said *butt* and not *ass* made it even funnier."

Uncle Joe looked at me with a straight face. "An ass is a domesticated member of the *Equidae* or horse family, called a jack."

He did not just say that. I couldn't think of a response.

We both started laughing and couldn't stop.

Finally, our hilarity subsided, and Uncle Joe looked at me, serious once more. "So now you know secret number five: *Make It Fun.* One of the secrets to success, and one of the laws of prospecting, is to always keep it fun. Prospecting is a hard and laborious activity, stressful and demanding. I have already explained to you the importance and necessity of building relationships. One of the keys to relationship building is to learn to laugh together.

"You tend to be driven, hardworking, and too serious. Having fun in business and life is not optional. It is critically important. Many fall into the trap of thinking that they will take time for fun, leisure, and pampering once they achieve wealth. Not true, Laura. What do you think comes first, happiness or success? We think that success will create happiness, but it is actually the other way around. Being happy creates more success, and in all areas of our lives."

"That makes sense," I said.

"Pop was a firm believer that if you didn't have fun, you'd go crazy."

I decided now was a good moment to put this secret into practice. I wanted to share more laughter with Uncle Joe. "What's one of the funniest stories you can remember from your days of prospecting gold?" I asked him.

He leaned back, looking up as he said, "Well, Pop told me a really funny one about Papa James and Uncle Bobby. You wanna hear it?"

"Yes, please."

"In 1855, there was a merchant named Crosby. An innocent, simple man, he was afraid of his own shadow and decidedly out of touch with his environment. One evening, Uncle Bobby, to make a little fun, invited this man to take a little walk in the outskirts of the town. Papa James and another man, hiding in wait for them to walk by, began shooting blank cartridges. Uncle Bobby fell, as if shot, and shouted, 'Git, Crosby! Git for your life.'

"Away poor Crosby ran, down the road, crying 'murder' at every jump. Then he rushed into the residence of Odell Jackson, declaring that Uncle Bobby had been killed and that he himself was mortally wounded. The poor, frightened fellow then threw himself on the floor, seeming to be seriously hurt. A doctor was summoned, who after giving Crosby a thorough examination, recommended a bath and a change of clothing."

I laughed and laughed as we made our way back to the front of the store. Frank and Matthew had already left. We locked up, piled into Uncle Joe's car, and drove home, continuing to take turns sharing funny stories. As we came close to home, Uncle Joe said, "Wait. I've got one more."

"Go ahead."

"When Papa James was prospecting in San Francisco, he and their crew, a number of Mexicans, relatives to Uncle Bobby's wife, Maria, used to stay out in the woods for days, or sometimes weeks, at a time. Uncle Bobby had a tent that he and my grandpa slept in, while the Mexicans stayed out in the open air, sleeping in blankets and huddled around a fire.

"One morning, the men were making pancakes in an oversized iron skillet when suddenly a jackass wandered upon their camp. Obviously, it had escaped from a nearby camp, and apparently it smelled the food. It approached the cooking area and buried its face in a bag of flour. The sounds of laughter from the hired men caused Uncle Bobby and Papa James to exit the tent, only to freeze in shock at what they saw. The jackass had left the flour bag to lick the pancake mix, and now the beast's face was covered with batter, drops trickling from his ears and chin.

"Papa shouted, 'GET!'

"The burro turned and bolted away, only to dash into the rope that was holding the tent upright. The spooked animal continued to plow forward, dragging the tent over. The Mexicans laughed and laughed as they watched Uncle Bobby and Papa pursuing their abducted tent into the forest."

"That's hilarious."

Uncle Joe laughed at my response, jerking the wheel unconsciously and sending us into the opposite lane.

I immediately reacted, shielding my eyes, lifting my legs, and planting my feet on the dash to brace myself for impact. When Uncle Joe veered back into our lane, I lost my balance. "Oh no!" I shouted as my skirt flew over my head, leaving my legs exposed.

As Uncle Joe slowed down, I heard a thumping noise. Uncovering my eyes, I saw Uncle Joe holding one hand on his stomach and pounding his other hand on the steering wheel as he laughed hysterically.

Uncle Joe kept trying to say something, but every time he did, he would recall my reaction and begin laughing again. He tried several times to get it out, but each time, he just laughed more wildly. His laughter became contagious, and I began to laugh uncontrollably too as I struggled to smooth my skirt and my dignity. The more I laughed, the more he laughed. And the more he laughed, the more I laughed. I laughed so hard that my stomach ached.

Finally, with tears streaming down his face, Uncle Joe looked at me and said, "Now *that*'s hilarious!"

12

Leaving a Legacy

EACH DAY THAT WENT BY brought a staggering increase in business. I was nervous at first, because I was a corporate girl, used to working for others and not myself. Before we opened, I had taken on the task of creating manuals and job descriptions, so that there would be uniformity in the workplace. It was a slow start at first, waiting for the sewing machines to arrive. It had not been easy to find a factory to produce them for us. Singer had its own factory, as did the Sears & Roebuck Company. The company we found was in South Bend, Indiana, but the production line only produced a hundred sewing machines a month, far below what we needed.

After six months of working with us, the manufacturer increased productivity to meet our orders. Our sales increased, and I was able to hire Sandy and Linda to help me. In the evenings, Frank would come to the storefront. We would eat dinner while I finished paperwork and continued to develop the business plan according to Uncle Joe's specifications. Frank and I had not set a date for our wedding yet, but we discussed it many times as I burned the midnight oil.

I wanted to implement the strategy of offering micro-business opportunities to other women, but I was concerned that our sewing machine distributor could not provide enough inventory. It would have to wait. However, I did install twenty sewing machines in the back room and started a sewing club. I called it Sew-n-Sow, a pun that, I hoped, would entice women to make their own clothes and connections while also having fun. Joanne and Angela took the lead role in that, and I was able to pay them a good amount for their services.

The front of the store had fifty chairs and a sewing station, where I did my demonstrations. Linda and Sandy handled the paperwork and referrals, just as they did before. Whenever I held a meeting, I would share my story before I demonstrated the sewing machine. I called my speech "Prospecting for Gold." Each time I shared it, the women's response was amazing; they seemed to enjoy every detail. I would include the funny stories and get everyone to laugh. Then I shared my grief over the loss of my mother and father, which usually brought tears.

After eight months, we were selling over three hundred sewing machines a month. Every day, I continued to prospect and sell. Frank tried to talk me out of going to the store every day, because the business was growing. He said I needed to focus on other parts of the business and let others do the selling. I knew someday that would come, but this was not that day. I hadn't forgotten Uncle Joe's advice. He had told me, "The biggest challenge for people in sales is that when they start to do well, they either slow down or get distracted, and they end up failing." I wasn't going to get distracted again.

But I was anxious to start the micro-business proposal, so Frank and I went to South Bend to discuss it with the manufacturer. We told him our business plan and estimated that, based upon our projections, we could sell as many as a thousand sewing machines per month. He was more than willing to accommodate us, but in order to fill orders of that magnitude, he would need a bigger building and more help.

We made several trips to other manufacturers in St. Louis and Columbus, Ohio, but between shipping and production costs, the increase in price would hinder growth and profitability. So we decided to go back to South Bend and see how we could develop a working relationship. The night before we left, Frank and I had dinner with Uncle Joe at the mansion. I still had my bedroom there, but due to the distance and late hours, I had rented a loft near the storefront for convenience.

Frank explained to Uncle Joe the dilemma we were facing, and told him that we were going back to our manufacturer, hoping to convince him to get a bank loan or government funding to build a bigger building. Uncle Joe listened carefully, and then asked, "Why don't you be the bank?"

Frank sighed. "We don't have that kind of capital."

"I do," Uncle Joe said as he took a bite of his apple.

I was stunned. "Uncle Joe, I could never—"

"Sure you could, and you can."

"But—"

"No buts about it," Uncle Joe insisted. "Laura, I have no children of my own. You and Matthew are heirs to all I own."

He opened his desk drawer and pulled out an envelope. Removing the papers within, he laid them on the table and said, "I have taken the liberty of setting up a living trust, and I want you to sign the paperwork as the trustee. You can use the funds to finance this new building, charge them interest, and make it a ten-year loan. That way, they will have time to build equity, get a loan from a local bank, and pay off the loan from you."

He handed me the paper and a pen. "Sign it and go do the deal."

"What about—?"

"Matthew?" Uncle Joe finished my sentence. "Matthew will take over the insurance company, and I have promissory notes that will roll over into his name at the time of my death."

"No time soon, I hope!"

"I haven't scheduled a date on my calendar, if that's what you mean," he laughed. "I mean to walk you down the aisle first, for one thing!" His expression turned serious again, and I could tell he was thinking about the business. Then his face lit up. "Frank, before you offer them financing for a new building, I've got a better idea. I think you should make them an offer they can't refuse. Tell them you are willing to finance, with collateral, but you want to know their net worth or buyout number. When they give you a number, offer them a cash price that is twenty percent lower, with a guarantee of continued employment for all employees and a five percent increase in their wages. Based upon what you tell me they are producing right now, I would estimate their net worth is probably around two hundred thousand dollars. You could purchase the company for a hundred and sixty thousand and own it debt free."

I didn't know what to say. Uncle Joe always managed to surprise me. He was clearly still thinking, the idea growing and developing as he shared it with us.

"Frank, do you know Bob Wilson at First National, on the East Side?"

Frank nodded. "I do. Our real estate company does a lot of business with them."

"Bob and I go way back. His dad used to own a hardware store on the South Side. When he sold it, he started a construction company, and I provided insurance for him for over twenty years. I never raised his rates, and Bob thanked me for it at his dad's funeral. He told me if I ever needed anything, to come and see him. Well, now might be the time to call in that favor."

"Yes, sir."

"If you can purchase this manufacturing company, I'm thinking you shouldn't use your own money to finance a new building. Use the bank's money instead. You can get a loan for the amount you will need with a two percent down payment, and at only 1.5 percent interest."

"Uncle Joe, I don't know what to say," I said. I was still in shock. In the space of a few minutes, I'd gone from owning a sewing machine sales company to potentially owning a sewing machine manufacturer.

"Name your first boy after me, Joseph Stephen Dunagan," Uncle Joe replied.

Why on earth? Well, if it'll make him happy.

"Joseph—it has a nice ring to it," I agreed.

Uncle Joe leveled a flat look at me. "Oh, Laura," he said. "Yes, sir?"

"I was kidding."

Uncle Joe pointed his fork at Frank. "Did you see that look? Laura's face was hilarious!" Then he winked at me, chuckled, and continued eating his dinner.

* * * * *

Frank and I went to South Bend, followed Uncle Joe's advice, and bought the company for one hundred and fifty thousand dollars. In less than a year, I had purchased a store and become a business owner, and now I had purchased a manufacturing company to build my own sewing machines.

We called Uncle Joe and told him the good news. It had been a long day and it would be a long drive back to the city, so Frank suggested we stay overnight at a local hotel and finish up the paperwork in the morning. He assured Uncle Joe he'd book me a separate room, and Uncle Joe chuckled, telling Frank that he trusted him to be a gentleman. The next morning, after we had breakfast at a local diner, we went back to our hotel, and Frank put in a call to Mr. Wilson at First National. When he got off the phone, he told me that the paperwork was already prepared and all we had to do was go in and sign. Uncle Joe had likely paved the way ahead of Frank's call.

We were enjoying our break so much that we decided to stay in South Bend for a few days and go to Fort Wayne to do some after-Christmas shopping. Sandy and Linda were more than happy to cover things while I was away, and they insisted that I stay and have a good time. After all, they said, I had not taken a weekend off since starting the business. I agreed and looked forward to spending a few days away from Chicago traffic.

The next morning, we found that an unexpected snowstorm had hit hard; ten inches of snow already lay on the ground, and the flurries were still falling like leaves in the wind.

We decided to wait it out. We had not brought clothes for a blizzard, so we rushed to a nearby Ben Franklin department store to purchase hats, scarves, gloves, jackets, and boots. By that evening, the town had shut down and the major roads were closed. We never made it to Fort Wayne.

Around 3:30 a.m., I heard a pounding on my door. I sat up and turned on the lamp. "Who is it?"

Frank's muffled voice came through the door. "Laura, it's me. Something's happened."

Still half asleep, I dragged on some clothes and opened the door "What is it?"

"It's Uncle Joe."

In an instant, I was fully awake.

"There's been an accident, and Uncle Joe is in the hospital."

"Is he hurt badly? Is he going to be alright? Who did you talk to?"

"Ellie Mae called the hotel. She didn't know much. She said Matthew was at the hospital, and he asked her to call us and tell us to come right away."

Due to the weather, a drive that normally would have taken one to two hours took us five. Matthew met us in the lobby and took us to the emergency room waiting area. The doctor had already made his rounds and explained everything to Matthew, but he was so distraught that all he could remember was, "Broken ribs, punctured lung—I don't know, Laura; he also said something about his heart—"

Matthew broke down then. He buried his head on my shoulder and began to cry. "Tell me he's gonna be all right, Laura, please."

I had never seen Matthew act like this—not even when Dad died. The last time I could remember seeing him cry was when he was nine and I had kicked him in the groin. I tried to be strong now for Matthew, but inside I was falling apart.

When I walked into the room, there lay Uncle Joe, looking like he had been in a boxing match with Jack Dempsey and lost, badly. His eyes were puffy and closed. A piece of white tape rested across his nose, and both his nostrils were packed  with gauze. Tubes were everywhere, and a putrid stench wafted from him. I could not bear to see him like that. I ran from the room, found a garbage can near the nurse's desk, and vomited.

Frank tried to comfort me, but I waved him off. I needed fresh air, so I went down to the lobby and walked outside. The cold, brisk air relieved my nausea, but not my sorrow. I closed my eyes, covering them with my hands. The frigid temperatures made my gloves feel like ice against my face.

"This is just a bad dream," I tried to tell myself. "It's just a dream." I kept waiting for Dad to appear in the dream and tell me everything would be all right. But Dad never came. This was not a dream.

I went into a daze then, reviewing my life from the first time I had ever seen Uncle Joe.

With his curled moustache and ridiculous suit, he had looked so out of place among the rugged men and tough women at Dad's funeral. The man I had initially despised, I had come to love. I couldn't bear to lose him too.

I looked around and saw an outdoor garbage can standing by the wall. I kicked it so hard, the lid flew off and trash splattered to the ground. The lid was still spinning when Frank came out to check on me.

"Are you all right?"

"No, Frank, my uncle is—"

Frank wrapped his arms around me and held me as I wept, my chest heaving and sobs catching in my throat. When my tears finally began to subside, he said, "He's awake. He wants to see you. But he's in bad shape, and his voice is weak."

Frank left me alone to go see Uncle Joe while he waited for Matthew. I went back to the room, looked in, and saw Aunt Debra close to Uncle Joe's bed. Somehow, I mustered up the courage to enter. He must have heard my footsteps, because his eyes opened as I approached.

"Hey, kiddo."

"Hi," was all I could get out without crying.

Aunt Debra moved back so that I could sit close to him, and I took his hand. "I can't lose you too! I just can't!" I cried.

He squeezed my hand to get my attention. I looked into his eyes then and read his lips, which said, "Come closer."

I bent down and placed my ear close to his mouth. His voice was clear, but weak and faint.

"I need you to calm down," he whispered. "I am weak, and I want you to sit close to me so I can give you secret number six."

"No, Uncle Joe, you can tell me when you get home," I said.

"Laura, I saw your dad last night. We were in the river together, panning for gold. He told me to come back to you, finish my task, and then return. He's waiting, so we need to hurry."

I did not want to hear that, but if Dad were actually with him, maybe hearing this would make me feel better. I sat down in the chair beside his bed and scooted close.

"Laura, life is short. It is here one minute and then gone the next—like a vapor. You need to enjoy it. You need to embrace it. You need to see when life is trying to teach you something.

"Did I ever tell you what initially inspired me to get into the insurance business?"

"No, sir."

"When your Aunt Debra and I were first married, we lived in a small apartment on the West Side. It was not in the best shape, and the property owner refused to fix the issues. Some years later, after I had graduated from law school, a few of the partners in my firm were having lunch, and the discussion of investments came up.

"The city was still under reconstruction after the Great Chicago Fire, and property values were low, making it a good time to invest. After some discussions, it was decided that several of the attorneys would purchase an apartment complex. One of them had a contact who was willing to sell, off the market, for the right price.

"It was that same apartment complex where Aunt Debra and I had rented while we were attending the university. Invited by these attorneys to participate, I agreed to invest and help purchase the apartment complex.

"About a month later, one of the tenants had a water leak that went undetected for four hours. The washing machine hose broke, and the water ran down into five units below. The damage would cost thousands of dollars to fix.

"When the apartment building had been purchased, one of the attorneys had set it up so that the owners were responsible for insuring the common areas, those that were used by all tenants, such as the hallways and stairs. For some reason, the insurance contract did not include damage caused by appliances. As a result, the damage caused by the leak was not covered by insurance, and the investors were required to pay for the repairs.

"When I investigated further, I learned that the insurance company had made a mistake; insurance on the appliances was required. The potential lawsuits were obvious, and I was afraid I would lose my investment.

"Looking back on how it happened, I realized something: We had been so anxious to purchase this building, we had all been working day in and day out, Saturdays and Sundays included, to secure the deal and close quickly. And then, I remembered number six of Pop's six secrets of prospecting: *Work Hard For Six Days, Rest For One.*

"It doesn't matter how things look on the outside. God created us all the same. We are going to face obstacles and be put through challenges. I wanted to be accepted by my peers, hoping that acceptance would open doors to be recommended, someday, for a senior partner position in the firm. Instead, by working every day, including Sunday, we were exhausting ourselves, and it cost us dearly.

"That day, I decided two things. One, I wanted to own an insurance company and, if possible, prevent something like this from ever happening again. Second, I decided from that day forward, I would never violate secret number six.

"Laura," Uncle Joe coughed. "I am so excited about your new business and so happy that you were able to purchase the factory. You have worked hard. Frank was not telling on you, but he said that you are working on Sundays, and I wanted to bring it to your attention. You're breaking secret number six, which is: *Work Hard For Six Days And Then Rest For One.*"

Instantly, in my mind, I saw Dad getting up daily before sunrise and going to the river six days a week, but never on a Sunday.

"I know that you are only trying to reach your goals, and that by working on Sundays, you mean no harm. However, if you do not follow this secret, you will burn out, lose out, and fall out before your time. Life is too short. You need to stop, learn to appreciate what you have, and cherish the days before they are gone. Otherwise, you grow old, look back, and have regrets, because all you did was work.

"I have many regrets in my life. I regret that so many years went by while I missed the first part of your life and Matthew's. I regret that Billy and I never had the opportunity to settle our dispute. For years, I remembered his last words: 'You are dead to me,' and 'I never want to see you again.'

"I regret that I never had children. I did my best to raise you like my own daughter. But you were Billy's child, not mine. I regret that your Aunt Debra never nursed an infant, changed a diaper, or taught a toddler to walk. I regret that I had to remove you from your friends and your life in Alaska. And I regret that you despised me for bringing you to Chicago—so many regrets."

Uncle Joe coughed again. "Despite my regrets, I have precious memories. Aunt Debra and I have traveled the globe. We were able to give to many charities, help the needy, and aid those less fortunate. The life I chose enabled me to seize those opportunities. Had I not observed this secret—work six and rest one—I would have burned out long ago. My health would have suffered; my decisions would have suffered; my marriage would have suffered; and all those people we helped over the years would have lost out."

Uncle Joe was quiet then. After a few moments, he indicated that he was thirsty. I got a cup of ice from the nurse and soothed his lips and throat. He licked his lips and nodded, signifying that he was ready to talk again. I leaned down, and he continued.

"Do you have a date yet? For your wedding?"

I thought I was going to fall apart when he asked me that. I remembered how he had said that he wanted to walk me down the aisle.

"No, sir, but we have been planning it."

"Frank is a good man. Marry him, and enjoy your life. Have children and raise them to follow the principles that were taught to you. Don't let life pass you by, or you'll miss out on what is most important."

Uncle Joe closed his eyes, opened them, then closed them again. I watched closely, and I could see he was still breathing. He opened his eyes once more and whispered, "At the end of the day, all you have is family. Cherish your family and you will live a full life, with no regrets." His eyes closed again.

I sat there waiting for his next sentence, until his breathing grew louder. Then he started to snore softly; he had faded off into sleep.

Exhausted now myself, I walked to the opposite side of the room and found a second chair. There was an extra blanket on it, so I covered myself up, sat back in the chair, and watched him sleep.

* * * * *

I woke up with a start. I looked over to Uncle Joe, but his bed was made up, and he was not in it. I panicked and rushed out to the nurses' desk, demanding that someone tell me where he was. Somehow, no one had noticed I was in the room, asleep in the corner. Uncle Joe had suffered a heart attack in the middle of the night and had been rushed to the operating room. But they'd lost him before he made it to surgery.

Uncle Joe was dead.

13

Pass the Torch

"ETERNITY IS WAITING FOR YOU," the minister said at the gravesite, closing his brief exhortation. He read Psalm 23, prayed a prayer of comfort for the family, and then invited guests to the mansion for a meal. Aunt Debra stood still as the minister shook her hand, then Matthew's and mine. Hundreds of bystanders stood and watched as the three of us each placed a flower on Uncle Joe's casket before walking away.

Aunt Debra was so strong throughout the entire process. She had picked out a beautiful navy blue casket, lined with white, plush, pillow-top cushions. Uncle Joe looked amazing compared to when I last saw him in the hospital. The cuts and bruises were unnoticeable. He was dressed in his favorite three-piece suit, with his gold pocket watch tucked away in its pouch. His handlebar mustache, coaxed with wax, was curled just as he liked.

Frank was so sensitive to my emotions, knowing when to speak and when to allow me to sit in silence, as was the case during the ride from the cemetery to the mansion. The reception was grand, with elaborate decorations, flowers, and mementos. A large portrait of Uncle Joe was placed on a luxurious gold easel in the foyer, near the large spiral staircase that led to the second floor.

There were mountains of food from some of Uncle Joe's favorite restaurants: delicious plates of *Hors d'oeuvres* generously served around the room, and banquet tables filled with fried chicken, roasted turkey, country ham, massed potatoes, fresh rolls, pineapple upside-down cake, varieties of ice cream, fruit cocktail, gelatin molds, and all sorts of scrumptious cake bites. The funny thing was, for health reasons, Uncle Joe had only eaten broiled fish, roasted chicken, salads, and fresh fruits and vegetables the last five years of his life. But this was how he would have wanted us to dine as we bid him farewell.

Losing Uncle Joe was as difficult, if not more so, than losing my father. I took the week off. I reflected upon his last words: *Work Six And Rest One.* Matthew and I stopped working on Sundays. Instead, we would meet and share a meal and reflect upon Uncle Joe's legacy.

Just as Uncle Joe had said, the promissory notes rolled over into Matthew's name, and he took over the insurance company. It was amazing to watch Matthew grow up so quickly, practically overnight. He handled himself and the company with dignity and pride.

The following Monday, I went back to work. Linda and Sandy ran the office. I just showed up to tell my story and give demonstrations of the sewing machines. I did not fall into depression, as I had before, but I struggled, at times, with Uncle Joe's absence. Going into his office was difficult for me, and I avoided it at all costs.

Aunt Debra already knew what was in his will, so it was no surprise to her how Uncle Joe had divided his funds and collections. The book, his prized possession, was willed to me: *The Greatest Prospector In The World.*

He made it plain that he wanted Matthew and me to remain in the mansion and tend to Aunt Debra as well as the upkeep. Frank and I discussed it and agreed that we would live there after we married.

One of the things that kept my mind off Uncle Joe's death was the continued planning for the wedding. Frank and

I decided to set the date for Uncle Joe's birthday, March 31. To make it easy, we chose to have the wedding and reception at the mansion. Ellie Mae and Linda were excited when I asked them to be bridesmaids, and Sandy was to be the matron of honor.

As we continued our Sunday tradition, we decided that, once a month, we would invite a special guest—someone who was close to Uncle Joe. Each visitor told us stories about him, and we cherished every memory.

First National approved the loan, and we were to break ground in April of that year on our new manufacturing plant. In the meantime, to keep up with production and increase our sales projections, we leased a large warehouse that was twice the size of the original building.

Knowing that we could supply the inventory, I presented the business strategy to several influential women of the city and to the women who had been volunteering for the past two years. I showed them how women could own their home businesses and sell sewing machines. I revealed the bonuses, benefits, and income structure for starting and developing a sewing machine home business. After the presentation, I had a question-and-answer time, which proved to be helpful. Based upon our discussions, I revamped and reorganized various aspects of the business proposal and was better equipped to explain and present the overall strategy. Once the system was complete and prepared, I set a date on which I was going to begin prospecting recruits.

Our wedding day came and went as fast as the Grand Prix. Frank and I went on a trip to Niagara Falls, planning to spend two weeks away, but we were called back early. The temporary facility had electrical issues, not detected at the inspection, which completely shut down production. Had we stayed away for two whole weeks, we would have lost a hundred and fifty sewing machines and been backed up with orders for two months, unless we paid overtime.

We arrived early Saturday morning by train. Frank left for South Bend and I went back to the mansion. The next day would mark exactly two months since Uncle Joe had passed, and Matthew and I agreed to continue our Sunday afternoon ritual. Since there was no time to invite a guest, we agreed that Ellie Mae, Mr. Robinson, and Miss Millie would be our honored guests. Ellie Mae and Miss Millie usually handled the cooking and serving, but not on this day. I contacted the chef from the Southside Café. He catered the meal, and his waiters served us. It was the first time the hired help had ever been in their leisure clothes and not their uniforms, while in the mansion. It was also a first for them to sit at the dining room table and be served a meal. I was delighted. It was only fitting that the people who knew Uncle Joe best were those who had worked for him for over twenty years.

Ellie Mae told many stories. Miss Millie only told two, and Mr. Robinson only one. We laughed. We cried. We reminisced about days long gone. It was a touching and emotional experience, and I cried so much that my eyes were swollen.

One of the stories Ellie Mae told us was a time when Uncle Joe was reading the newspaper and drinking his coffee, as he did each morning. It was a Sunday morning, she said, when he was reading the "funnies," his favorite—*Winnie Winkle the Breadwinner.* He started laughing so hard that he knocked his hot coffee over, and it spilled on his trousers. Feeling the intense heat, he removed his suspenders and lowered his trousers in an attempt to prevent the scalding coffee from burning his thighs. Hearing the commotion, Ellie Mae rushed to his aid, only to find Uncle Joe skipping and hopping around the office with his breeches to his ankles and his underpants exposed.

I thought about that story later in the day, and it gave me the courage to go into his office for the first time since his passing. When I reached for the doorknob and looked at the sign, I could recall the first time I snuck in. On this day, I walked the same path, viewing the same pictures as the first time, one by one.

I walked over to the oval table, and there sat the book, encased in its shrine like a pharaoh in his tomb. For some reason, Uncle Joe's absence lessened the excitement I felt as I read again the words on the cover: *The Greatest Prospector In The World.* I had no desire to touch it that day, although I was faithfully implementing the six secrets in my life and in my business. I felt lost and alone. I remembered Dad saying, "Turn the bad into good," but I could not find any good in Uncle Joe's absence.

I went upstairs to wait for Frank to come home. I lay in bed, opened the nightstand top drawer, and retrieved my notebook of goals. I read the front page and started to think about what I had written that day. *Who is the special person I am to mentor?* I flipped through the pages, reading the goals until I dozed off.

Deep in sleep, I dreamed a special dream. I was at the river, at the same spot that I had visited in my previous dream—my favorite spot, where Dad and I spent so much time. I walked around a tree and standing there were Pop Angus, Dad, and Uncle Joe! I could not hear what they were saying, but I could tell that they were teasing one another, because I could hear them laughing jovially.

All three were wearing their waders, bib overalls, and personalized hats. I looked down at myself, but I wasn't wearing my waders or my bib overalls. I was wearing my Mary Jane shoes, my free-flowing, pleated black dress with the V-neck white collar. A snug leather belt sat around my waist, matching my navy Newport Matinee hat, decorated with a white daisy on the side.

I could tell that Pop Angus was ribbing Dad and Uncle Joe. I moved closer, wondering what was happening and how I had got there. Just then, Pop saw me out of the corner of his eye. He turned and looked me up and down, his eyes shining with pride. "Why, Laura, don't you look mighty fine today!"

Dad and Uncle Joe spun around, and they both smiled when they saw me.

"We were just talking 'bout you," Pop said, and he spit a wad of tobacco to the ground. "Ain't dat right, boys?"

"Sure is."

"And she's just as pretty as the day I last saw her," Uncle Joe added.

Pop Angus smiled. "I was telling my boys how it is up to you to pass the torch! That's right! You're the one who will carry on the tradition." He turned to Uncle Joe. "Joseph, you gave her the book, right?"

"Sure did, Pop," Uncle Joe replied.

It was strange hearing them talk. I recognized Dad's voice and Uncle Joe's, but it seemed that they talked funny— almost as if their accents were more distinct when they were around Pop.

"Laura, it's your responsibility to pass on the six secrets when the *right* person comes along. Don't look for that person; that person will find you—whoever it is."

"That's right, Laura," Uncle Joe added. "Just as it was with you and me. I had no idea you were the one. I thought it might be Matthew, but it wasn't—it was you! I just had to wait for you to discover yourself, before you were ready for the six secrets." Uncle Joe lifted his arms, stretched them wide, and said, "And just look at ya now: so pretty, smart, and sassy!"

Dad, Pop Angus, and Uncle Joe started laughing. I ran and embraced Uncle Joe with a tight squeeze, something I did not get a chance to do before he passed.

Dad chimed in. "Uncle Joe has told me about everything you've done, and I cannot tell you how proud I am of what you've become."

I started to cry, and transferred my hug to Dad. How I missed them both!

"Don't cry, pumpkin, it'll be all right. You'll see. You'll accomplish your task, and someday we'll be together again."

A fog descended, creeping down the river, and it separated me from the three of them. When it lifted, I was alone on the bank. Pop, Dad, and Uncle Joe were back in the river, walking upstream together. It was a grand sight to see, and one that I could never forget.

Just before they were out of sight, Pop Angus turned around and said, "Get ready, she's coming soon!"

She? Who is she?

14

What's Next?

"AND THEN I WOKE UP," I said as I reached across the bed and tucked Mary in. I was exhausted and ready to call it a night.

"What's next?" she asked.

"Aren't you tired yet?"

"No, Mommy ... What happens next? Tell me. Please tell me the rest of the story!"

"I don't know. It's kind of boring from here, even for a ten-year-old girl." I wanted to convince my daughter to let me finish it another night. Every night, for the past seventeen days, Mary had begged me to tell her stories so she could learn more about my life, her grandpa, Uncle Joe, and my dad's family. Bit by bit, I shared episodes from my journey, from the early days on the river to my upbringing in Chicago, along with my struggles as a female salesperson and my success as a prospector that came from the six secrets Uncle Joe had taught me.

I laid my head down on the pillow and pretended that I was asleep.

"Mommy, you tried that last night ... It's not working!"

"It's not?" I asked, as I popped open one eye.

"No, and it didn't work the night before that either!"

"Oh, all right," I said as I sat up. "I'll continue."

"What happened after you woke up from the dream with Pop Angus, Papa Billy, and Uncle Joe?" Mary asked intently.

"The following morning, I took my notebook and wrote down the dream—every detail. From that point on, I started a journal, documenting my journey. I decided to go back and write out all the events from my beginning days with Dad in Alaska to my life at the mansion in Chicago. It took me five weeks, two hours a night, to pen my voyage.

"I launched a second business called Dunagan Enterprises and started teaching women who wanted to become business owners. Their initial payment provided them with a sewing machine at half the cost to make one, a teaching-training manual, and a systematic guide to prospecting, referrals, and recruiting, with a lifetime membership to the Sew-n-Sow® catalog that featured patterns, sewing tricks, and techniques for beginners and novices, with contemporary styles for all ages.

"We finished building our new manufacturing facility, and within a month, Dunagan Textiles had distributed over five hundred sewing machines! Two months after the new building was completed, we sold a thousand sewing machines in one month. At the beginning of our second year in business, I had already prospected, recruited, trained, and licensed over one hundred and ninety-five new owners.

"At each meeting, I continued my tradition of sharing a ten-minute version of my story. I was holding two workshops a week to train people and we had outgrown the storefront training space. Your daddy spoke with Jorgy to see if any of the other storefronts had leases near termination and, if so, would there be a possibility for Dunagan Textiles to place a bid for a vacant storefront. The only lease coming to its expiration date was the Top Hat Cleaning store, but it was four months away, and Thomas Turner had not renewed his lease.

"Your daddy and I discussed our options, and we had no choice but to contact some nearby hotels to rent space. For the next four months, we were able to rent the ballroom at the

Elms Hotel at an incredible price because the hotel had just gone through bankruptcy.

"In addition, Daddy was able to negotiate a deal with the owner of the Pioneer Arcade for the Top Hat Cleaning storefront. Jorgy and Mr. Turner had a falling out over Turner's mistreatment of a waitress, who happened to be Jorgy's mistress at the time. So he strong-armed Turner out of the lease.

"We immediately started remodeling the space for more seating, but the attendance at the Elms Hotel meetings continued to grow, and the 450-seat ballroom could house more than the two storefronts combined. So we changed the plans and remodeled the old Top Hat Cleaning storefront into a showroom and another training center.

"As the business expanded, my reputation grew. I did not plan it. It just happened. I was being invited to speak at various events and organizations and eventually started the U.S. Council for Women Entrepreneurs (CWE). Just as Uncle Joe predicted, in 1934, I made the cover of *Time* Magazine as a pioneer in women's business ownership.

"During this time, your dad and I were so busy building the business and traveling that we chose to wait before having children. Although we knew the risks of having a child later in our lives, we felt it was better not to have children while we were so absorbed by our business. Then the day came when I received the news—you were coming!

"I was excited, but a little scared too. Nine months later, you were born at 6 lb., 8 oz. We named you after my mother, and you were the most adorable girl in the world—to me anyway!"

"Thank you, Mommy." Mary wrapped her arms around me.

"You're welcome, sweetheart," I said, as I turned to the final page in my journal.

"Through a twenty-three-year career of selling, I became the first female business owner and millionaire in Illinois. Some said that I became the envy of, and example for, women entrepreneurs all over America. That may be a little over the top, but

I am humbled. Years later, people asked me how it all happened and where I learned to do what I do. Each time, I answered, 'It's a secret, and I have six of them! And those who know the secrets will become the greatest prospectors in the world.'

"Okay, baby, it's time to go to sleep. Story time is over."

Mary looked at me. "I want to know the six secrets. Can you teach me to be a great salesperson?"

Mary's words brought to mind my dream, and Pop Angus saying, "Laura, it is your responsibility to pass on the six secrets when the right per-son comes along. Don't look for that person; that person will find you."

Tears started streaming down my face. I looked down at my young daugh-ter and said, "My dear, I'm not going to teach you to sell. I'm going to take you to Alaska and teach you to pan for gold."

Afterword

I first decided to create this story five years before I finally published it, but the ideological conceptions included in this book began much earlier. I started adulthood as a police officer in Canada. During those early days in policing, I had the opportunity to specialize in the science of interview and interrogation, which began a lifelong fascination with how people think and behave and how to build relationships. In particular, I studied Neuro-Linguistic Programming (NLP), an approach to communication, personal development, and psychotherapy created by Richard Bandler and John Grinder in California in the 1970s.

After the birth of my children, Matthew and Laura, I left policing to pursue a better, more prosperous life for my family. Since then, armed with a high school education, some police experience, and a deep understanding of relationship building, I have been able to start businesses in property management, finance, direct sales, and publishing industries. These businesses have yielded hundreds of millions in gross revenue as they have grown around the world. Although I could never take credit for the successes of these businesses on my own, I can claim that I prospected and recruited all of my original partners in those businesses, convinced them of a vision for our joint success, and led the sales forces in those companies. For me, it has all been about prospecting.

As I entered my tenth year of entrepreneurship, I found myself teaching prospecting and sales training all over the world. While at an event at the Hard Rock Resort in the Dominican Republic with the top leaders of a Norwegian gourmet espresso company called Zinzino, I started to train the leaders by telling a wild, adventurous tale of little Laura in the rivers of Alaska. By that time in my life, I had been deeply impacted by Jim Stovall's blockbuster *Ultimate Life Series,* and Og Mandino's classic book *The Greatest Salesman in the World.* In the weeks following my time in the Dominican Republic, I realized that I was going to write this fiction book to illustrate my greatest prospecting lessons, and in doing so, I would honor Mandino and Stovall for their contribution to my life.

Throughout the story, you likely learned several important lessons that will, if practiced, lead you to higher levels of success in sales:

1. *Dress For The Weather:*

   • Present the best "you."

   • You never get a second chance to make a first impression.

   • Remember, you are the product.

   • Look good, sound good, smell good.

   • People don't buy from you until they like you.

2. *Know What You're Looking For:*

   • In sales, realize that if you are selling to everyone, you are selling to no one. Create a profile of the best customer.

- Figure out where those customers are.

- Prospect where you know the customer is going to be.

- Get the guts to ask for referrals; a happy customer will always refer.

3. *Use The Right Tools:*

  - Be organized.

  - Keep notes and journals; use software.

  - Realize that you, your sales techniques, and your story are your greatest tools.

  - Know how your product works, and be a product of the product.

4. *Get In The River, Even When You Don't Want To:*

  - Prospecting is not easy; keep doing it even when you are not having success.

  - Keep doing it even when you are having success, or if you are having a good day.

  - Keep prospecting!

5. *Make It Fun:*

  - Nothing worth doing is ever easy.

  - The bigger the goal, the bigger the challenge.

  - Find the humor in what you do-a great laugh will cure the common cold and cause you to enjoy what you do.

6. *Work Hard For Six Days, Rest For One:*

- This has been my hardest lesson and is easily the biggest secret.

- In the books by Og Mandino, Dale Carnegie, Jim Stovall, and in all the lessons of life, there are constant reminders to take time to regroup.

- In the words of Nike: Just do it!

Our family has been blessed to see the wealth of the world because of these six secrets. They are my gift to you.

In the story, I have created a wonderful tale that follows the classic hero's journey. Laura is an inspiration to us all, but that doesn't mean her circumstances mirror ours. At a couple of places, I actually departed from reality, and I want to take a moment to speak to this. Having a rich uncle sure does make life easier and makes for a better story, but it is not a real reflection of what most of my readers are likely to go through. Most of us are out there doing it on our own. Most of us did not have a rich uncle or wise mentor. Be assured, the advice revealed in this book still works even without a rich uncle. The book can be your guide.

In addition to the six secrets that the story reveals, there are a couple of extremely important points that need to be summarized and woven into your plan if you dream of becoming *The Greatest Prospector In The World*:

1. *Vision:* In Chapter 12, Laura talks in detail about what the vision is for her company. She talks openly to her followers about what the world will be like. This common trait is seen in the world's elite influencers. My favorite story of "vision casting" is the Steve Jobs legacy. Now, there was a man who could see the future. If you are serious about changing your life, then

tell people about it. When you publicly announce how the world will be when you are successful, you will attract other people to you, and at the same time you will force yourself to stay the course.

2. *Set an example:* Throughout her life, Laura remained focused on prospecting. Even when she was successful, she stuck with it. By ensuring that her followers saw her continuing to prospect, even at times of high success, she set the ultimate example. In your life, once you determine the right behavior for success, keep doing it. You will be tempted to stop or slow down. Don't.

3. *Plug In to Prospecting:* I have a deep desire to help entrepreneurs all over the world to become Great Prospectors. Every one of us has the ability to be great. Let this book be the beginning of your journey toward prospecting mastery. There will be other books in this series. I am now traveling the world looking for modern-day examples of *The Greatest Prospectors In The World,* and one day those examples will be a book. In the meantime, get plugged into our community at www.greatestprospector.com.

I hope Laura's story has inspired you to become one of *The Greatest Prospectors In The World!*

Ken Dunn